P9-CFJ-651

Christmas the World Over

Books by the Author

GARDEN FLOWERS IN COLOR
VEGETABLE GARDENING IN COLOR
ANNUALS FOR YOUR GARDEN
GARDEN BULBS IN COLOR
LITTLE SAINTS OF CHRISTMAS
THE CHRISTMAS TREE
CHRISTMAS IN THE GOOD OLD DAYS
GROUND COVERS FOR EASIER GARDENING
TOYS THROUGH THE AGES
EASTER GARLAND
    (WITH PRISCILLA SAWYER LORD)

Christmas Crib in Canterbury Cathedral.

Courtesy The British Travel Association.

Christmas the World Over

How the Season of Joy and Good Will
Is Observed and Enjoyed
By Peoples Here and Everywhere

By DANIEL J. FOLEY

Illustrated · Line Drawings by CHARLOTTE EDMANDS BOWDEN

CHILTON BOOK COMPANY
Philadelphia   New York   London

J 394.268
F   C.1

LAKEWOOD MEMORIAL LIBRARY
LAKEWOOD, NEW YORK 14750

Dedicated to
Katherine Van Etten Lyford

Copyright © 1963 by Daniel J. Foley. First Edition. *All Rights Reserved.*
Published in Philadelphia by Chilton Company, and simultaneously in
Toronto, Canada, by Ambassador Books, Ltd.

Second Printing, October 1964
Third Printing, April 1966
Fourth Printing, July 1967

Library of Congress Catalog Card Number: 63-21171
Manufactured in the United States of America by
Quinn & Boden Company, Inc., Rahway, N. J.

In Appreciation

To my family and to countless friends and associates who have endured Christmas talk in season and out, I am most grateful.

To Mrs. CHARLOTTE EDMANDS BOWDEN who has catered to my many whims by delineating in line the spirit of Christmas in the various countries of the world.

To Mrs. LORRAINE I. CRABTREE, Miss MARGARET M. FOLEY, and Mrs. JOAN BAILEY for typing the manuscript. Also, to Mr. PAUL CRABTREE and the Misses MARCIA and CAROL CRABTREE for their assistance.

To Mrs. PRISCILLA SAWYER LORD for research, for advice on technical and editorial details, and for verification of numerous items of information gathered from her extensive library. Also, for reading the manuscript and planting countless ideas in my head.

To Miss KATHERINE VAN ETTEN LYFORD for permission to use her manuscripts on Latin American Christmas customs and for the generous contribution she has made to this book by interviewing students from the various Latin American countries to correlate numerous traditions and folkways not generally known or recorded in English. Also, for extensive research in the field of folklore, customs, and manners.

To Miss MARGARET BRINE for material and observations gathered in her extensive travels in many parts of the world.

To Mrs. VIRGINIA C. SHATTUCK for permission to use her manuscript on Mexican Christmas customs.

My hearty thanks to the following libraries, organizations, and individuals for the use of research material, photographs, and information on customs and folkways in various countries:

Mr. HANS AANSTED
THE ABBOT MEMORIAL LIBRARY
Miss LILLY ABBOTT

Mrs. MARY C. BLACK
THE BOSTON ATHENAEUM
Miss EUNICE BROWN

Miss Marjorie Cawthorn
Mrs. James D. Chesterton
Dr. and Mrs. Timothy F. Clifford
Mrs. Dorothy Cooke
Corning Glass Company
Cybis, Inc.
Miss Lillian De Houx
Miss Maxime De Houx
Mr. Cesar Delgado
Miss Linda Delgado
Mr. Rolando Diaz-Maestre
Mr. Rick Eaton
The Essex Institute
Miss Winnifred Foley
Mrs. William W. K. Freeman
Mr. Edmundo Gavassa
Mr. Paul E. Genereux
Mrs. Yolanda Molina de Goldman
Mr. Leopoldo Guinand
Mr. Federico Gutierrez
Miss Margaret Hackett
Rev. Stanley S. Harakas
Miss Joan Hardy
Miss Helen Harvie
Mr. Theodore Hebert
Mrs. Donald Hunt

Mr. Jorge Laso
Dr. George L. Laverty
Mr. John Lee
Sister M. Gratia Listaite
Mrs. Henry Cabot Lodge
Miss C. Sally Low
Mrs. Margarita de Macaya
Mr. Alegria Moscoso
The New York Public Library
Mr. Mariano Ospina-Hernandez
Mr. Claudio Campbell Pena
Miss Ester Posada
Miss Luz Posada
Mrs. Amelia S. Rawding
Mrs. Frances Dianne Robotti
Mr. and Mrs. John P. Roche
The Salem (Mass.) Public Library
Mrs. Mary Scrimshaw
Mrs. Nevin Scrimshaw
Miss Susan Scrimshaw
Mr. Julio Silva
Mr. George Taloumis
Mrs. Maria Elena de Valle
Rev. Francis X. Weiser, S.J.
Wenham Historical Society
Mrs. Francis R. Williams

Especially to Mrs. Barbara Woll and Mrs. Dorothy Maciejowski for the stimulus which they provided in assembling the notable and comprehensive exhibition, "The Crafts of Christmas Around the World," held at the Wenham Museum in 1961.

Daniel J. Foley

Salem, Massachusetts

6

Introduction

At Christmas, more than at any other time of year, nostalgia rules human hearts. This age-old season of rejoicing, essentially a festive time for children, is also the one great occasion of the year when adults return to the realm of childhood. Often, this return is merely a fleeting glance backward to those golden carefree years which can never be recaptured. To the current generation of teen-agers, this colorful season is but a fleeting part of growing up, while to younger brothers and sisters Christmas is an interlude of wonder, of delight, of excitement—and sometimes of disappointment. In any event, it is a time filled with anticipation and high hopes.

The manner in which folk customs and traditions have evolved to embellish the simple story of the birth of the Christ Child is indicative of the importance of Christmas in the hearts of men. Through ritual and ceremony, the captive appeal of music and song, the gastronomic approach of feasting and fancy cookery, and the dynamism of drama and pageantry, the Christmas season has developed into a spectacular manifestation of life at its richest.

It used to be a long way to Bethlehem in Judea from almost everywhere. But that storied land is very close to us today. And so, too, are the countless colorful folkways that have clustered around the ageless story of the birth of the Christ Child over the centuries. The people of every country where Christianity has made its spirit felt have woven and rewoven the simple story of the Babe of Bethlehem. They have embraced their own folk life to interpret, to explain, and to recall with vivid reality the incidents relating to the King whom they have made their own.

By no means are all of the ways in which men express their joy best suited to an appropriate observance of Christ the King's birthday. The abuses that some people criticize today parallel in many ways the offenses their forefathers condemned centuries ago. Indeed, the weaknesses of humanity show themselves conspicuously on festive occasions, and not the least of these is Christmas.

In weaving together the story of Christmas as it is observed the world over, not all the fascinating details can be recounted in a book this size. This account, then, is concerned primarily with those folkways which still exert a major influence on this glorious feast of the hearth, the heart, and the home. Many old customs have pre-Christian roots stemming from several countries. Others have been so skillfully blended and adapted by a number of countries as to be less easily linked to one particular nation in their present form. It is not so much where they originated, but rather the meanings they hold and the pleasure they give that concern us.

In bygone days, social customs provided pleasant pastimes for countryfolk, and many of these customs were linked with agricultural pursuits which have largely disappeared. However, not all of our traditions can be traced to rural life. There were those peculiar to town and city life, the Court, the University—in fact, to every phase of existence relating to the professions and the trades.

During the past half-century, as the pattern of life has changed, the outlook of the typical rural dweller and that of his city cousin have been affected immeasurably by modern methods of travel and education, and by rapid advances in the world of science. Thus, it may be said that this is hardly the day of the simple man; rather it is an era of sophistication. The trends which have changed the outlook of the farmer, the townsman, and the city dweller have, at times, made the past seem more remote than is actually the case.

Nonetheless, tradition dies hard, and discerning people everywhere are aware of the fact that many popular folk practices and usages contain the very essence of history. Currently, there is a revival of interest in folk music, folk art, and folklore which provides a new kind of perspective on the past. This revival has sharpened our senses and made us cognizant of the lure of things old and quaint as they once related to everyday life. To be sure, many folkways have never been entirely forgotten—in fact, some of them have been revered and enjoyed for so long a time that they remain today as pleasant links with the past. Or, are they merely "innocent associations of a simpler, perhaps happier, time"? Whatever the reader's reaction, surely even those strange notions once held sacred by our forefathers have added luster to the seemingly logical manifestations of mood expressed by ancient rites, usages, and observances. The highly graphic accounts that remain testify that they were both pleasurable and amusing, and afforded a welcome contrast to an otherwise mundane, routine way of daily life.

Even in this atomic age of constant change, many evidences of ancient Christmas customs remain. Bringing in the greens, although they are not now gathered in the manner they once were, is an inseparable part of gracious living with roots traceable to truly pagan origins. There is something so festive about the placement and the manner of decorating with fragrant boughs of foliage and bright berries that, whatever its original significance, it has become an almost universal practice by second nature. Even when artificial materials are used, the effects are not without appeal, and the pleasure of decking the house has not lost its meaning.

There are perhaps not enough adequate words that express the essence of Christmas—Joy, Peace, Good Will, Delight, Happiness, Hope—yet, they all convey something of the spirit of the season. Nor do there seem to be any actually new thoughts, or ways of expressing them, that have not been chronicled previously.

8

The approach in *Christmas the World Over* has been to assimilate the solid core of tradition and folklore with sufficient detail to provide a representative picture in words and sketches of how Christmas is lived, observed, and enjoyed around the world.

Using the typical signs and symbols associated with Christmas and combining with them their own native folk motifs for embellishment, children and grown-ups, down through the ages, have given expression to their imagination in countless forms and patterns. A piece of wood, a handful of straw, a lump of clay, an old tin can, or bits of colored paper—whatever is available—all provide the raw materials for many of the handcrafts best loved and most greatly enjoyed in this machine age. These commonplace materials, transformed by skilled handwork, often emerge as objects of great beauty. They are, in essence, the enduring links in the age-old chain of tradition which we cherish as did our forefathers in earlier generations. Thus, the crafts of Christmas from the various countries of the world have a charming quality and display a great warmth of emotion and the joy of good work.

The objects thus fashioned, be they crude or elaborately made, are best compared to hymns of praise, for they express in their own inimitable way the joy that is Christmas. That they appeal primarily to the childlike instinct which is part and parcel of all of us bespeaks their charm and gives true meaning to the event they commemorate: the birth of the Babe of Bethlehem, whose natal day calls for gifts—the best one has to offer.

In every corner of the world where Christmas is celebrated, families look forward to this festive season with keen delight as they unpack their treasured Christmas keepsakes and baubles to deck the family tree, to add luster to wreaths and garlands, and to bring sparkle and brightness to every part of the house. The individuality expressed in those bits and pieces which are home-made often provide the best part of Christmas.

As Americans, we are the beneficiaries of Christmas customs and traditions from every part of the world. It is our heritage to assimilate, to observe, and to enjoy these hallowed old-time practices so rich in meaning, in symbolism, and in nostalgia. To know them and to seek out their significance is to enjoy Christmas to the fullest.

DANIEL J. FOLEY

Stjärngossar på Skansen. The Swedish custom of the *Stjärngossar*—Star Boys—who, clad in white, go from door to door singing their songs, dates back to the Middle Ages. The boys represent the Wise Men of the East and their attendants. One, dressed in black and carrying a money-bag, represents Judas. Nowadays, the old custom is rarely kept up, but the songs are well known to everyone. *Courtesy Swedish National Travel Bureau.*

Santa Claus at Selfridge's in London. *Courtesy British Travel and Holidays Association.*

Offering the lamb at Midnight Mass in the Church of St. Michael of Frigolet at Arles, in the south of France, is one of the delightful old folk traditions still observed in this ancient city. *Courtesy French Cultural Services.*

Midnight Mass on Christmas Eve in Arles means that everyone is dressed in the best tradition of the countryside. The *fougasse* cake is a gift to be left at the manger. *Courtesy French Cultural Services.*

Contents

IN APPRECIATION 5

INTRODUCTION 7

CHRISTMAS THE WORLD OVER . 13

ASIA MINOR 17
Bethlehem 17

UNITED STATES . . . 19

EUROPE 25
Austria 25
Belgium 27
Czechoslovakia . . . 28
Denmark 31
England 33
France 42
Germany 48
Greece 53
Holland 57
Ireland 62
Italy 63
Norway 70
Poland 73
Russia 74

EUROPE—*continued*
Scotland 76
Spain 78
Sweden 84
Switzerland 90
Wales 95

LATIN AMERICA . . . 96
Brazil 100
Chile 101
Colombia 102
Costa Rica 103
Ecuador 104
Guatemala 106
Mexico 108
Peru 113
Puerto Rico 113
Venezuela 115

ASIA 120
China 120
Japan 121

AUSTRALIA 123

INDEX 124

Adoration of the Shepherds. A detail from an eighteenth-century Neapolitan panorama, portraying the birth of Christ.

An eighteenth-century household Christmas crib made by a German sculptor, Johann Georg Dorfmeister.

Christmas the World Over

Christmas is known by a variety of names in various countries. In Latin, it is the Feast or Birthday of Our Lord. The word *Christmas,* meaning the Mass of Christ, closely resembles the Dutch *Kersmis.* When spelled *Xmas,* X represents a similar Greek letter which translated into English is pronounced "Ch," with a hard sound. The German term *Weihnacht,* which means sacred night, refers to Christmas Eve, *the* holy night. In France, *Noël,* which means birthday or news, is commonly used. *Yule,* derived from the Scandinanvian tongue, may refer to the turning of a wheel, as the rising of the sun-wheel after the winter solstice. Some claim that it comes from an old Anglo-Saxon word meaning feast, referring to the celebration of the winter solstice.

It was in the first quarter of the fourth century A.D. that the date December 25th was established at Rome as the official time for the observance of the birth of Christ. However, many Eastern churches differed on the date, and it took nearly a hundred years for the celebration of Christmas, as we know it, to become adopted, but the communicants of the Greek Orthodox Church still follow the practice of observing it on January 6th.

Christmas occurs between two great pagan festivals, the Saturnalia and the feast of the Kalends. Through the centuries, this festival of Christmas has naturally retained some of the earmarks of each of these ancient celebrations. The Saturnalia, extending from December 17th to December 24th, was an age-old observance in tribute to Saturn, the god of plenty or bounty. Even as we observe Christmas today, it was a time of rejoicing, hilarity, feasting, and merrymaking. All work ceased, children were released from customary discipline, ill will was forgotten, and even wars ceased at this season of the year. Evergreen boughs and berries were brought indoors to deck homes and thus dispel the gloom of winter. The exchange of presents was a common practice. Little clay dolls, toys, and a wide variety of trinkets were sold at fairs. Good fellowship as manifested in the warm greeting of friendship was the spirit of the times. What Charles

13

LAKEWOOD MEMORIAL LIBRARY
LAKEWOOD, NEW YORK 14750

Dickens expressed in the nineteenth century was a kind of reaffirmation of a universal spirit that is as old as civilized man.

In pre-Christian times, one day during the festivities was set aside to pay tribute to the birth of the Unconquered Sun; this occurred at a time corresponding to the Christmas season as we know it. It was the most important feast of the Mithraic creed, the state religion of the Roman Empire, and the competitor of budding Christianity. Another feast that occurred at this time of year was the Cleansing of the Temple, in the latter part of December. The significance of this occasion must not be overlooked, since the followers of Christ had previously professed Judaism and the dedication of the temple was a rite they had known for centuries.

In adapting some of the practices of all these festivals, the early fathers of the new Christian church captured the spirit of the festival, which was rebirth, and transformed it to signify the coming of Christ; thus, an ancient festival was given a new meaning. In the cold North, the Teutons observed the winter solstice, calling it *Yule*. Since the nights were long, it was referred to as "the twelve nights."

In early January came the Kalends, marking the beginning of a new year. This was a time for elections to public office, also for feasting and merriment. The comic note was personified by amateur actors known as mummers, who dressed up in grotesque costumes made of animal skins and paraded through the streets. The spirit of the occasion was best exemplified in the exchange of wishes for happiness and prosperity, a custom which lingers on in our New Year's activities today.

Libanius, a famous scholar of the early church who recorded his impressions of the season nearly sixteen hundred years ago, makes us realize that human nature has not changed materially. He wrote: "The festival of the Kalends is celebrated everywhere as far as the limits of the Roman Empire extend . . . The impulse to spend seizes everyone . . . People are not only generous themselves, but also towards their fellow men. A stream of presents pours itself out on all sides . . . the Kalends festival banishes all that is connected with toil, and allows men to give themselves up to undisturbed enjoyment. From the minds of young people it removes two kinds of dread: the dread of the schoolmaster and the dread of the stern pedagogue . . . Another great quality of the festival is that it teaches men not to hold too fast to their money, but to part with it and let it pass into other hands."

In the beginning, Christmas was essentially a day of spiritual observance, without any of the fanfare and color now attending it. There were neither carols nor bells, nor were there any gaily decorated trees or elaborate spreads on the banquet table. "It was a feast of the senses and a feast of the soul. Bethlehem, bathed in supernal light, was the exclusive object of wonder."

With the passing of the centuries, men have been inclined to forget the true significance of Christmas, blinded by the glitter of tinsel, the brilliance of light, the feasting, and the gift-giving that have come to surround this holiday. Thus, we do not always hear the angels sing nor do we see the true beauty that surrounds and envelops the Nativity at Bethlehem.

14

The Wise Men are seen everywhere in Spain at Christmas. Here they are visiting a hospital.

Feeding the birds with a sheaf of grain on a pole is a part of Christmas in Scandinavia.

The *triggel*, a Swiss Christmas cookie, made in superbly carved wooden molds, is edible sculpture at its best. *Courtesy Prints Division, New York Public Library.*

This straw Christmas ornament of intricate design is a fascinating example of Norwegian peasant craftsmanship. *Courtesy Norwegian Information Service.*

Christmas decorations in the Della Robbia manner by Julia S. Berrall are popular in the United States. *Courtesy John Roche.*

Asia Minor

Bethlehem

In 1865, Phillips Brooks, founder of Boston's famed Trinity Church in Copley Square, made a trip to the Holy Land and was deeply moved by what he saw. It is believed that the words for "O Little Town of Bethlehem," one of the best-loved carols of American origin, were written in his notebook in the fields outside Bethlehem where he walked on Christmas Eve. This is the image of the birth-place of the Christ Child held by millions.

O little town of Bethlehem
    How still we see thee lie!
Above thy deep and dreamless sleep
    The silent stars go by.
Yet in thy dark streets shineth
    The everlasting light;
The hopes and fears of all the years
    Are met in thee to-night.

For Christ is born of Mary;
    And gathered all above,
While mortals sleep, the angels keep
    Their watch of wond'ring love.
O morning stars, together
    Proclaim the holy birth,
And praises sing to God the King,
    And peace to men on earth.

How silently, how silently,
    The wondrous gift is given!
So God imparts to human hearts
    The blessings of His heaven.
No ear may hear his coming,
    But in this world of sin,
Where meek souls will receive him still
    The dear Christ enters in.

17

Where children pure and happy
   Pray to the blessèd Child,
Where misery cries out to thee,
   Son of the mother mild;
Where charity stands watching
   And faith holds wide the door,
The dark night wakes, the glory breaks,
   And Christmas comes once more.

O holy Child of Bethlehem,
   Descend to us, we pray;
Cast out our sin, and enter in,
   Be born in us to-day.
We hear the Christmas angels,
   The great glad tidings tell:
O come to us, abide with us,
   Our Lord Emmanuel.

With the passage of time and the strife that has been rampant among men down through the ages, the little town of Bethlehem has changed considerably in the past two thousand years. As a result, many of the visitors who travel to the Holy Land today are disappointed in what they see, for they have conjured up in their mind's eye a picture of a Bethlehem which does not exist.

The great Basilica or Church of the Nativity and the numerous buildings that serve as headquarters for various religious organizations belong to a much later era. However, the Shepherds' Field, Jaffa Gate, the hills of Judea, Rachel's Well, the River Jordan, and other familiar landmarks help one to visualize some of the landscape as it probably was at the time of Christ's birth.

In Bethlehem, Christmas is observed on three different dates. For most Christians, the day is December 25th, but followers of the Greek Orthodox Church, the Syrians and the Abyssinians, who have never accepted the Gregorian calendar, cling to January 6th, "Christmas old style." The members of the Armenian Church, on the other hand, celebrate on January 18th—Epiphany, according to the Julian calendar.

Every year, on Christmas Eve, people from all parts of the world converge on Bethlehem to witness the religious ceremonies, the Procession and the Mass, and to get a first-hand view of the place where the manger stood. Each and every visitor takes away with him highly personal impressions of what he has seen and felt. Reactions vary, but, in any case, the significance of the occasion transcends all that men have done to preserve and to perpetuate the site and the surroundings of the crude cave where the Christ Child was born. Those of us who cannot make the journey must be content with the superbly phrased verse of Phillips Brooks'—

O little town of Bethlehem,
   How still we see thee lie!
Above thy deep and dreamless sleep
   The silent stars go by.

18

United States

The story of Christmas in the United States of America can be told in many ways. In capsule form, it might read like a series of newspaper headlines ranging from top billing on page 1 to the sports columns.

It was on Christmas Day in 1492 that Columbus made his first settlement in America on the northern coast of the island of San Domingo. The *Santa Maria* had been wrecked because the vessel had struck a sandbar, but Columbus and his crew were rescued by the natives. To honor the Feast of the Nativity, and as a tribute of gratitude for having escaped from the shipwreck on Christmas Day, Columbus named the fortress and the adjacent village "La Navidad," the Spanish words for "The Nativity."

On December 25, 1621, Governor Bradford of the Plymouth Colony found it necessary to reprimand several young men who had arrived recently from the ship *Fortune* because they refused to work on Christmas Day. In Bradford's journal is a detailed account of the affair: "On ye day called Christmas day, ye Govr. caled them out to worke (as he was used), but the most of this new company excused themselves and said it went against their consciences to worke on ye day. So the Govr. tould them that if they made it a mater of conscience, he would spare them till they were better informed. So he led away ye rest, and left them; but when they came home at noone from their worke, he found them in ye streete at play, openly: some pitching ye barr, and some at stoole-ball and such like sports. So he went to them and took away their implements and tould them that it was against his conscience that they should play and others worke. If they made the keeping of it a matter of devotion, let them kepe their houses, but ther should be no gameing or revelling in ye streete. Since which time nothing hath been attempted that way, at least openly."

From the spectacular point of view, especially as regards outdoor illumination and decorations, the United States leads the world in Christmas showmanship. In the realm of commercial activity, no other nation anticipates Christmas for

19

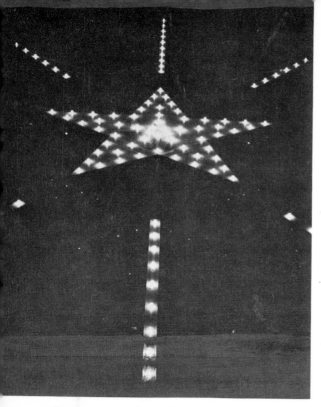

Star on top of South Mountain at Bethlehem, Pa., visible for many miles around. *Photo by W. W. Wehr. Courtesy of the* Globe Times, *Bethlehem, Pa.*

The Christmas Tree on the White House grounds at Washington, D. C. *Courtesy Mrs. Warder I. Higgins.*

Beating the drum for Old Christmas. Miss Elvira Payne is the official drum beater for the Old Christmas celebration held each January 5th at Rodanthe on North Carolina's Hatteras Island. Her older brother, the late Daniel B. Payne, was official drummer for many years, and she inherited this honor upon his death in 1954. The cloth and wood figure known as "Old Buck" is, like the drum, a traditional feature of Old Christmas. The whereabouts of the ancient drum and of "Old Buck" between Old Christmas celebrations is a closely guarded secret. *Courtesy North Carolina News Bureau.*

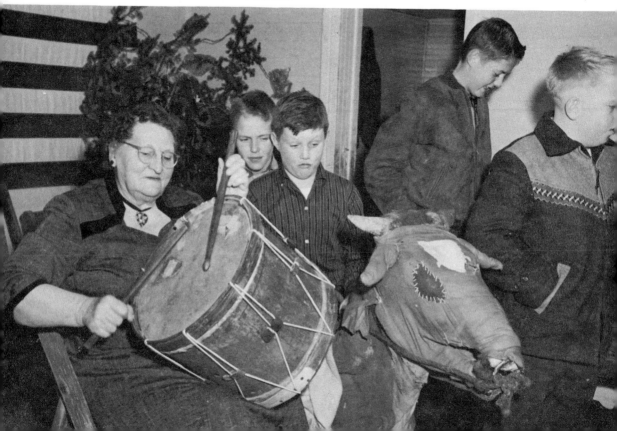

so long a period with so much sharply focused advertising. The excitement and the rustle and bustle that attend Christmas on every level of American life out-distance that of practically every country in the world. This is said not in a boasting manner, but rather to illustrate the way in which Christmas in our country has evolved since the close of the Civil War. Uncounted millions of Christmas cards, yards of ribbon and wrappings, and all the trappings of the holiday season are mass-produced to such an extent that Christmas is becoming perhaps too much standardized.

On the other hand, nowhere else in the world within the boundaries of a single nation is Christmas observed with a greater variety of customs and traditions. Every country and practically every region of it has descendants here. Within the past two decades, removed by only one or two generations from life in Europe, many of our citizens have shown a growing awareness of their cultural heritage. In their desire to preserve it, they are rediscovering and reviving old folkways, modes, and manners of doing things that have given tradition itself a new kind of significance. Their enthusiasm is imbued with great reverence, a sense of devotion, and a love for the ways of the past.

However, this is not to say that contemporary happenings and new ways of observing and enjoying Christmas are being ignored. Santa Claus, the Christmas tree, poinsettias, Christmas cards, carols, the immortal message of Dickens, and a host of other holiday diversions—all contribute to making our Christmas a time of great exuberance and joy. Throughout all the states—in public displays, in churches, in private homes—manger scenes are enjoying an unprecedented wave of popularity. Despite the glamour of the community Christmas tree, amid the gleam of electric lights and all the outdoor pageantry Christmas in millions of American homes across the land is essentially a feast of the heart and the hearth as elsewhere in the world. Within the confines of the family circle, it glows and shines as it was intended that the birthday of the Christ Child should be celebrated. Grandma's recipes for cookies and cakes are cherished and often shared. The sentiment linked with ornaments treasured from year to year is akin to that shared by people the world over. Churches and Sunday schools make the true meaning ring as they compete with the activities of the mercantile world. Nevertheless, the same excesses and distortions that plagued our forefathers are still with us.

In Boston, New York, Philadelphia, Cleveland, Dallas, and Baton Rouge—from San Diego to Seattle, from Denver to Atlanta—everywhere that one turns the distinct flavor of Christmas as formerly enjoyed somewhere in the Old World is emulated and loved. However, it is in city neighborhoods, in suburban communities, and in small towns that the spirit of Christmas is felt most intimately. Wherever people are closely linked by common interests, the feast of Christmas burns with an especially bright glow and rings with a trueness of tone that is easy to sense. Christmas Eve on Boston's Beacon Hill, with its bell-ringers and carol-singers, its softly lighted windows and garlanded doorways, is vivid enough to make one feel that Charles Dickens himself might be giving a reading of the *Christmas Carol* in some nearby auditorium as he did a century ago.

A visit to Duke of Gloucester Street in Williamsburg at Christmas carries one back to eighteenth-century Virginia since the flavor of an old English Christmas

21

A costumed couple performs dances in the eighteenth-century manner for Yuletide visitors to historic Williamsburg, Virginia. This informal performance, being presented in front of Chowning's Tavern on Duke of Gloucester Street, is but one example of the many holiday activities in the restored city. The Christmas traditions of George Washington's day are observed in Williamsburg during a fortnight of celebrations. *Courtesy Colonial Williamsburg.*

Bringing in the Yule Log is an ancient tradition revived in Williamsburg, Virginia, during the fortnight of holiday celebrations. Hundreds of visitors join in the Yule Log ceremonies and taste of the "wassail" bowl on Christmas Eve. *Courtesy Colonial Williamsburg.*

'Tis the season to be jolly. Costumed carolers give forth with song in Williamsburg, Virginia, during the fortnight of Christmas festivities celebrated in the colonial manner with Yule Log ceremonies, the firing of the Christmas guns, the Royal Governor's Reception, and the lighting of the community tree. *Courtesy Colonial Williamsburg.*

The Sun. The set piece, often used at Christmas in displays of fireworks by Colonial Williamsburg, is based on two eighteenth-century sources: a print of fireworks, dated London, 1763, and Diderot's Encyclopedia. *Courtesy Colonial Williamsburg.*

has there been preserved in all its colorful detail. In this same community, the lighting of the Christmas tree, inaugurated in 1843, brings back memories of nineteenth-century Christmas. Pennsylvania offers the Moravian observances at Bethlehem and Lititz, the Mummers' Parade on New Year's Day in Philadelphia, and the Christmas yards or *putzes* of the Pennsylvania Dutch.

The Christmas tree, introduced to America by the German settlers of this commonwealth in the eighteenth century, has become our national symbol of Christmas. Perhaps our country's most distinct contribution to the Christmas traditions of the world is the community Christmas tree found in nearly every city and town, large and small, all across the country, and in the elaborate lighting effects on buildings, trees, and shrubbery seen everywhere. Little else that we enjoy at Christmas can be called truly American in origin, since our Christmas heritage is a composite of that of the whole world.

Santa Claus is so much a part of North American childhood that young folk consider him a family friend who lives at the North Pole and makes an annual visit to boys and girls everywhere with the aid of his countless helpers, all dressed alike, who appear in department stores, schools, and even Sunday schools. It is well known that he came to America with the Dutch who settled New York in the seventeenth century; at this time he was called St. Nicholas. Actually, his popularity in the United States stems from "A Visit from St. Nicholas," written in 1822 for the amusement of his own children by a New York clergyman, Dr. Clement C. Moore. The account as presented in the author's *Toys Through the Ages* brings to mind the highlights of the story:

"In 1809, Washington Irving had told the story of St. Nicholas in his *Knickerbocker History,* for the delight of readers in England and America. Some time later, in 1821, a small juvenile was published in New York called *The Children's Friend.* It was a simple book, with eight sparkling color plates and an equal number of verses about 'Santeclaus,' who was shown riding in a sleigh drawn by a single reindeer. This is believed to be the first mention of Santa's reindeer and sleigh, as we know them today.

"Undoubtedly, Dr. Moore had read Irving's book, for it became popular at a time when there were few American writers, and he may have been familiar with *The Children's Friend.* At any rate, he wrote 'A Visit from St. Nicholas,' one of the best-loved and most widely quoted poems ever produced in America. Yet, at the time, he thought it of little merit. To a scholar of Hebrew who was working on a dictionary in that language, a man who was also a distinguished Episcopal preacher and the son of the Bishop of New York, it probably seemed like doggerel. It was simply a bit of verse to delight his own children, and the story was based on his own family and their surroundings.

"Clement Moore's St. Nicholas was no austere saint, such as was portrayed in the Old World Dutch tradition by Washington Irving. Rather, he was a jolly fat man, typical of the prosperous Dutch burghers who had settled New York nearly two centuries earlier. In fact, this inimitable characterization may well have been inspired by a real person, whose name was Jan Duyckinck. He was the caretaker at the Moore home in New York, and it is claimed that he was 'fat, jolly, and bewhiskered' and that he smoked 'a stump of a pipe.' Dr. Moore's St. Nicholas had eight reindeer, each with a name, to enable him to get around in his wonderful sleigh.

23

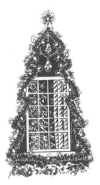

" 'The Night Before Christmas,' as the poem is fondly referred to, would surely have been forgotten or lost, had it not been for Miss Harriet Butler, the daughter of a clergyman from Troy, New York, who was visiting the Moores that Christmas and heard the clergyman read his poem. She got permission to copy it in her album and, the following year, it appeared anonymously in *The Troy Sentinel,* just before Christmas. However, it was not until 1837, when it appeared with a collection of local poetry in book form, that Dr. Moore acknowledged that he was the author. Curiously enough, that same year Robert W. Weir, professor of art at West Point, painted a portrait of Santa Claus, fat and jolly, about to go up a chimney after filling the stockings he found there.

"The story of Santa's phenomenal rise to fame in the years that followed and his versatility in meeting the requests of children all over the world have been told in scores of books. However, there is more to the story of this wonderful poem. During the latter years of his life, Dr. Moore lived in a large, rambling farmhouse in Newport, Rhode Island—which is still standing. Each year at Christmas since 1954, James Van Alen, a native of this historic community, has presented a dramatic reading of 'A Visit from St. Nicholas,' assisted by his wife and four children from the neighborhood. Dressed in costumes of the period, the group assembles in front of the fireplace of the Newport house for the reading of the poem. Then it is re-enacted in the yard, under floodlights, for the pleasure of the neighbors, followed by carol singing. Later, gifts from the sleigh, which arrives on a float, are distributed to a local children's home. Jimmy Van Alen, as he is popularly known, has organized the House of Santa Claus Society, and hopes to be able to raise enough funds to make the Moore house a historic shrine and Christmas Museum. This enthusiastic champion of Dr. Moore believes that no American has provided more joy for young and old. Mr. Van Alen has written a sequel of seventeen couplets to the poem, because, as a child, he thought the poem ended too soon, and he wanted 'to make the fun last longer.' In an interview with Charles D. Rice, he added, 'I used to worry about Father, standing there by the open window as the poem closes. I was afraid he might catch cold, so now I've tucked him safely into bed. I hope Dr. Moore isn't cross at me.' "

Europe

Austria

From the time that St. Nicholas and his companion, Krampus, arrive until Epiphany, January 6th, when the Wise Men appear, there is one long month of excitement and joy for the children of Austria. The Christkind (Christ Child) brings them their gifts on Christmas Eve and he even helps to decorate the tree. These people have carp for supper on the festive evening and their bounteous dinner on Christmas Day with roast goose and all the fixings is similar to the food served in other European countries.

In Austria, many of the folkways, enjoyed for centuries, have been preserved and adapted to contemporary life. Tradition dies hard even under oppression and war, especially in countries where there are many isolated villages. There, the simple pleasures of life are limited to the entertainment which the people provide for themselves. As a result, in these far-off places, customs dating back to the Middle Ages have been nurtured and preserved for posterity.

Tracing the carol tradition in the countries of Europe from the time of St. Francis and Jacopone in Italy, through succeeding centuries, we find in Austria a heritage of Christmas folk music rare in its charm and beauty. As Clement Miles reminds us in *Christmas in Ritual and Tradition:* "In Carinthia in the early nineteenth century, almost every parish had its local poet, who added new songs to the old treasury. Particularly popular were the *Hirtenlieder* or shepherd songs, in which peasant worshippers joined themselves to the shepherds of Bethlehem and sought their devout emotions. Often these carols are of the most rustic character and in the broadest dialect. They breathe forth a great kindliness and homeliness.

> Rise, shepherds, though the night is deep,
> Rise from your slumber's dreaming!
> Jesus, the shepherd, watch does keep,
> In love all men redeeming.
> Hasten to Mary, and look for her Child,
> Come, shepherds, and greet our Saviour mild!"

25

LAKEWOOD MEMORIAL LIBRARY
LAKEWOOD, NEW YORK 14750

The refrains of many of these simple songs are delightful imitations of the sounds emanating from shepherds' instruments. Although they are not lost, the pity of it is that few of these truly melodious gems are seldom heard except in Austria. In recent years, however, the widely known Trapp family has introduced some of the choicest to North American audiences.

Because of her great love for song, the musical tradition of Austria is unusually rich and varied. There are carols for every mood which express the joy of Christmas, and they resound from every mountain village and valley town in this country where the very joy of life has been a well-practiced art for centuries. Thus, we find shepherds' carols, lullaby carols, companion carols, dance carols, star carols. Those who have the talent enjoy yodeling as "a natural way to honor the Divine Child." They pour forth their hearts before the crib or out of doors where their clear tones and the spontaneous melodies literally fill the air with joy.

It was in 1818 in the Alpine village of Oberndorf that Franz Gruber, a school teacher, and Father Joseph Mohr, the village priest, produced one of the best loved of all Christmas hymns: "Silent Night! Holy Night!" Although the story of this beautiful carol has been related many times, like the story of Christmas itself, it is ever fresh and inspiring.

Few Christmas historians have a greater love for the lore of Christmas than Francis X. Weiser. In *The Christmas Book,* he tells of the Austrian companion carols: "An extremely interesting group of songs—mostly German—wherein the singer represents himself as accompanying the shepherds, or as taking their place, addressing the Child, or Mary and Joseph, in a simple, affectionate manner. Often a broad local dialect is used, as in the old Austrian carol from the Tyrol, *Jetzt hat sich halt aufgetan das himmlische Tor* (The gates of heaven's glory did spring open suddenly). Here is a rollicking, joyous stanza:

> So came we running to the crib,
> I and also you,
> A bee-line into Bethlehem,
> Hopsa, trala loo:
> 'O baby dear, take anything
> Of all the little gifts we bring:
> Have apples or have butter,
> Maybe pears or yellow cheese;
> Or would you rather have some nuts,
> Or plums, or what you please.'
> Alleluja, alleluja;
> Alle-, Alle-, Alleluja."

"In with the good luck; out with the bad" is the spirit in which misfortune is smoked out of house and stable at this time of year. The animals are blessed and fed extra portions of food. The "smoke blessing," as it is called, is also given to each member of the family by the head of the household. Greens of many kinds are enjoyed both for their beauty and as signs of hope for the forthcoming spring; besides, they have a particular significance in banishing the demons that lurk in the darkness during the gloomy days of winter. The tip of a spruce or a fir tree was often decorated with colored paper, nuts, and apples, and then hung upside down in the corner of the best room, which was referred to as "the Lord God's Corner."

26

While kissing under the mistletoe is believed to be distinctly English in character, a custom long known in parts of Austria was often enjoyed at inns and taverns where people spent New Year's Eve. Greens were used to decorate the rooms and a large wreath was hung from the ceiling in the parlor or largest room. Lurking in a dark corner was a strange character known as Sylvester, ancient and ugly in appearance. He wore a flaxen beard and a wreath of mistletoe on his head. Whenever anyone in the room—man or woman, young or old—passed beneath the evergreen wreath, this old man would jump out from the shadows and bestow a rough kiss and a hug on the passer-by. But, when midnight came, Sylvester was driven out. This folkway is believed to represent the banishing of the old year.

Belgium

In Belgium, St. Nicholas makes two visits: the first on December 4th to check on the children's behavior and the second on his feast day, two days later, when he fills their shoes and baskets with the candy and the toys they have long anticipated. Belgian children make every effort to remind the good saint where they live by leaving a generous supply of hay, water, and carrots for his horse (or donkey) near the door of their houses. When they awaken on December 6th, they know immediately by the disorderly appearance of their rooms that he has paid them a visit during the night, because everything is topsy-turvy. For those whose behavior has been less than good, the gifts are switches, which no one looks forward to with any enthusiasm.

Christmas Day in this small country is essentially religious in nature, with the children forming processions on their way to church. As they march along, some carry religious figures while others display little shrines and crucifixes decorated with ribbons and streamers. One of the neighborhood boys dressed in appropriate costume appears as St. John the Baptist. He leads a white lamb and carries a crucifix. Church bells herald the paraders, the clergy participate, and there is plenty of spirited band music on their way as fond parents gaze in admiration at the younger generation attired in its Sunday best. Since many customs have been adapted from their German neighbors, the Christmas tree is a popular fixture in Belgian homes. So, too, are the candy and gingerbread images of St. Nicholas, as well as many other signs and symbols of the season.

Formerly, strange antics were the order of the day on the feast of St. Thomas, December 21st. Not only did the children lock out the schoolmaster until he promised to treat them, they also tied a rooster and a hen by the legs and then allowed them to escape, following which the children scrambled to catch them. The girl who caught the hen was called the "queen"; the boy who captured the rooster was known as the "king." In some communities, children locked out their parents or the servants. Schoolboys even bound their teachers to chairs and carried them to the local inn, where the luckless schoolmasters could pur-

27

chase their liberty only by giving their scholars the refreshments of their choice. This bit of old-time horseplay was common in many parts of Europe.

In Flanders, planning for the Christmas season means hours of rehearsing for the plays which are an integral part of the great feast day there. They are sponsored by the churches in the various villages and the parishioners take great pride in performing, since the leading actors are chosen with the greatest of care. The children of the parish school who are selected portray the choir of angels. The plays vary in each community, and characters are introduced in accordance with the whims of the villagers. Hence, it is not unusual in one of the border towns, where smuggling is a rather common practice, for a poacher or a smuggler to appear, bearing his gift to the Christ Child.

As in Provence, where gypsies are always included among the *santons* in the manger scene, the Flemish people believe that there is room at the crib for all who wish to come—even known sinners—since the Christ Child offered salvation to all who sought it. In presenting Nativity plays in Flanders, it is an old tradition that each of the characters taking part must resemble one of the picturesque figures found in Brueghel's paintings. This requirement not only limits the use of costumes to those worn at the time, it also sets the spirit of the acting of these fascinating plays in a true sixteenth-century atmosphere.

In *Christmas Customs Around the World,* Herbert H. Wernecke writes that it is customary "for each village in Flanders to appoint three men who have the privilege of walking along the streets dressed as the Magi. In order to receive this appointment the men must have been outstanding for their practice of virtue during the preceding year. Attired in their robes, they make their rounds and sing two songs at the door of each home in town. One song describes the journey of the Magi. The other is the Flemish version of 'O Tannenbaum.' At the end of their two songs the Magi are usually invited in for a cup of tea or some pancakes. It takes a hardy trio to keep up with the demands made on their appetites and their capacities. Yet, this is Christmas to Flanders, where old traditions survive."

Czechoslovakia

A thousand years ago, there lived in Bohemia (as Czechoslovakia was formerly called) a prince named Wenceslaus, who was heir to the throne. In those days, wars and family feuds were as commonplace as the cruelty associated with human turmoil. Wenceslaus, not wishing the throne, preferred to remain a duke, so was murdered by his mother and brother because they wanted him to ascend the throne. Actually, he was a person of contemplation, deeply moved by Christianity, the new faith he had adopted. His good deeds became widely known even before his death, and eventually a hymn was written in tribute to him in his native land.

Four hundred years later, Elizabeth, the daughter of the English King James I, was betrothed to the King of Bohemia. At the time, troops of French and English

28

soldiers were sent to Bohemia to champion widely different causes. It is said that the French soldiers brought back the cravat (the necktie knotted in the Croatian manner), then a new fashion in men's attire, whereas the English came home singing "Good King Wenceslaus," a hymn in honor of a hero of their princess' adopted country. At least, this account of the origin of the popular Christmas carol has been advanced by Michael Harrison in *The Story of Christmas*.

In Czechoslovakia, the Christmas season begins with Svaty Mikalas Day on December 6th, and all the ceremony and fanfare associated with the feast of St. Nicholas elsewhere in Europe are traditional here.

It is believed that St. Nicholas descends from heaven on a golden cord accompanied both by an angel garbed in white and by a devil called Cert, dressed in black, who carries a whip and rattles a chain to remind children who have misbehaved of what awaits them. This medieval image of Saint Nicholas has outlived even those who tried to banish the custom, several hundred years ago.

In Czechoslovakia, December 24th, 25th, and 26th are the holidays of the winter season. December 25th and 26th are state holidays, known as First and Second Christmas. After the festive meal on the "Generous Eve," the decorated Christmas tree, usually a fir or a spruce, is lighted. Under it gifts from family and friends are assembled, ready for distribution.

Setting up Christmas cribs or "Bethlehems" is a favorite pastime with families in Czechoslovakia. In the mining district around Pribram, making and collecting figurines has always been a most engaging hobby since, in bygone days, the miners were accustomed to long periods of unemployment. Their Bethlehems were complete village scenes carved from wood or fashioned from bread dough and then elaborately painted. The ingenuity and the workmanship displayed in these large Nativities resulted in artistic creations of extraordinary merit and great beauty. In addition to the familiar crib setting, there were the peasants and tradesmen taken from real life—bakers, butchers, night watchmen, miners, shepherds, and the like. Although some Nativity scenes or individual figurines were the work of professional craftsmen, most were made by members of the average family who enjoyed carving and sculpture. The Bethlehems created through the years have expressed a truly realistic attitude toward life, reflecting both its misery and its beauty.

While the Christmas tree has its place in Czechoslovakian Christmas, its use is only a little more than a century old. Decorations used to be very simple, especially among poor families, but they were always natural and unusually artistic. Apples, pears, prunes, nuts, home-baked pastries cut into a variety of shapes, gingerbread, and clippings of colorful paper and cloth material—all were typical. However, with the development of the glass industry, handsome baubles and ornaments of every conceivable kind were used on Christmas trees in Czechoslovakia and shipped in great quantities all over the world.

Since Christmas occurs a few days after the winter solstice when night is longer than day, there is a popular saying in Czechoslovakia that "The day the Lord is born we are a flea's step ahead." Hence, this turning point in the farmers' yearly routine has always represented a time of promise for the future. With more sunshine ahead, the time for planting crops to replenish the disappearing

29

food supply was approaching. This accounts for a number of superstitions, old notions, and folk beliefs associated with this season, all of which were aimed at creating favorable conditions for the success of the forthcoming harvest and an abundant livelihood for the people.

It was customary to take a part of every course of the Christmas dinner to the animals—to the cows so that they would give more milk; to the hens so that they would lay all the eggs needed; to the pigs so that they would fatten properly. Bones from the meat course of the Christmas dinner were buried under the fruit trees in the garden to assure a plentiful crop during the coming year. Another old practice required the farmer and his wife to go into the garden before Christmas dinner and shake the fruit trees, all the while expressing the hope that the trees would bear well.

Incense was burned in the house and in the barn to keep evil spirits away. An ancient tradition in Bohemia, long forgotten now, was a masquerade party similar to the custom now observed during Shrovetide.

Methods and procedures for foretelling the future are among the most ancient of customs in many parts of Europe. On clear evenings, the girls went to gaze into deep wells or into the water (through broken ice) in ponds and rivers, looking for the image of their future husband. Sometimes they shook the fence or the lilac bush in the garden and then waited to hear the barking of a dog; from the direction where the bark was heard, their future husband was sure to come. This ritual was accompanied by a rhyme: "Shaking, shaking the lilac bush, tell me, little dog, where my beloved one eats tonight."

When the dishes were removed from the table following Christmas dinner, time-honored beliefs provided amusement for young and old. One custom was to cut an apple in half to foretell the future from the picture presented by the core. If the core revealed the shape of a cross, it signified an unfortunate fate for the person who cut the apple, while the outline of a star meant a happy future. Other methods of divination involved pouring hot lead into water, or floating walnut shells with little candles on water in a washbasin, or throwing shoes over one's head.

Of ancient lineage in Czechoslovakia, in Poland, and in parts of Germany is the practice of forcing cherry blossoms into bloom for Christmas. At the beginning of Advent, a branch from a healthy tree is cut and placed in water in the kitchen. The flowering branch serves not only as a foretaste of spring but also as a beautiful decoration for Christmas. Even more important is the fact that, if the branch blossoms forth on Christmas Eve, good fortune is in store for the maiden who cut and cared for it: she is sure to find a good husband within the year.

Christmas foods include *calta,* a plaited white bread, baked to a golden crisp, and sometimes called "Christmas bread." A well-known street in Prague—Celetna—took its name from this "fast" food since it was on this street that many bakers had their shops. Carp has long been a favorite holiday dish, as well as *cuba* (a pudding made of peeled barley, boiled in milk, buttered and baked with mushrooms). *Masica,* or fruit stew (consisting of dried pears, apples, prunes, nuts, and raisins) is served with a slice of Christmas bread. In a country like Czechoslovakia, where farming is an important occupation, many other traditional dishes make Christmas a bounteous feast.

"On St. Stephen's Day there is no master" is a popular expression still heard in Czechoslovakia. Formerly, poor children went about singing carols, hoping for gifts of money to assist their families. In many parts of Europe, this was the appointed time for farmhands to leave their employers and seek work elsewhere. Thus, a generous parting gift was given to each departing worker. "Stephening" meant singing and dancing and feasting, and a toast was drunk "to new blood" on this day.

Denmark

The Danes, too, make Christmas Eve their greatest festive event of the year and share the heritage common to all Scandinavia—chiming church bells, an elaborate dinner, the ceremony around the Christmas tree, and soul-stirring hymns and carols in their candle-lighted churches.

The Danes refer to Santa Claus as the "Yule Man," but it is their beloved *Nisse,* the gnome of Christmas, who is the center of attention for both young and old. With warm pride they point to the contributions of Christmas lore made by such illustrious sons as Hans Christian Andersen, Jacob Riis, and Einar Holboll, a modest post office clerk, the originator of the Christmas seal.

The imprint of Christmas registered so indelibly in the heart-warming stories of Washington Irving and Charles Dickens in the nineteenth century had its counterpart in Hans Christian Andersen's "The Fir Tree," "The Little Match Girl," and other enchanting tales. It was the fir tree who wondered, "Was I really born to such glorious destiny?" This and dozens of other much-loved tales of the inimitable storyteller have made Christmas an unforgettable day for millions of children in all parts of the world for more than a century. It was Andersen himself who once wrote, "Life itself is the most wonderful fairy tale of all." He was always filled with that child-like sense of wonder and it showed itself in everything he wrote. When Jacob Riis came to America at the turn of the century, he recorded many of the customs of his homeland for American readers, thus making them familiar with the lore and the customs of the Scandinavian region.

During the past half century, Denmark has given valuable keepsakes to the world in the form of beautiful blue-and-white Christmas plates made of porcelain. Produced by two of the nation's leading manufacturers, the plates carry motifs true to the spirit of Danish Christmas. It is said that the popular demand for these plates grew out of a practice followed by the wealthy of giving plates of cookies and fruits as gifts to their servants. The plates on which the gifts were offered were frequently of much better quality than anything the servants owned, so they hung these tokens on the walls of their homes, thus starting a collector's trend. As a result, this Christmas hobby became world-wide and a new industry was developed in Denmark.

All nature is glorified at the Christmas season. Both birds and animals receive fitting attention in the way of food. Bits of suet and bread are hung on trees

31

and the best of the sheaves of grain which were selected at harvest time are put out. These picturesque sheaves perched on spruce poles are placed in many locations around the farm or home grounds near the gate, on the corner of the barn, or even on the roof. When birds come to eat in great numbers, a year of hope with good crops is foretold. During this season, fish and game are undisturbed by traps, nets, and snares, and farm animals receive extra portions of food with the wish, "Eat well, keep well; this is Christmas Eve."

As the family sits down to dinner on Christmas Eve, the Christmas fire, *Julebaal,* a relic of pre-Christian times, is lighted in the open where it can be viewed from indoors. The glow on the hearth, the gleaming candles, and the bright-eyed Danes who observe the season in all its joy and glory point up the importance of light, warmth, and friendship, which are the dispellers of gloom, evil, and trouble among men. In olden times, even the turning of wheels was frowned upon at this season lest impatience be displayed to the sun whose rising position in the sky denotes the coming of another spring. The lighted candle in the window gives the universal message, "Welcome, stranger," and means that food and shelter are offered to travelers who may be passing—all in the spirit of the Christ Child.

Christmas Eve dinner starts with rice porridge sprinkled with cinnamon, and containing the magic almond that one of the family is sure to find in his serving. Roast goose stuffed with apples and prunes, served with red cabbage and small caramel-browned potatoes, is the favored holiday dish. So, too, is apple cake, made with layers of bread crumbs, applesauce, and jam topped with whipped cream. Marzipan and many kinds of cookies—including the *Brunekager,* flavored with molasses and spice, peppernuts, and other favorites—are made in generous quantities to be served to everyone who comes to call during the holidays. No good housewife fails to show her guests true hospitality lest one should "bear the Yule spirit from your house" since it would not return for a whole year. Early in the month, baking day is the time when most of the delicacies are prepared since certain kinds of dough must be allowed to "ripen" before baking.

In some parts of Denmark, a group of village musicians climb to the church belfry to "blow in the Yule." Despite the cold weather, they play four hymns for each of the major compass points, followed by the ringing of the church bells.

After dinner is over and the dishes are washed, expectation runs high among the young ones. Father and Mother disappear into the locked parlor, light the tree, and open the door. Then all clasp hands and circle around the tree, singing some of the old Danish Christmas hymns, among them "Merry Christmas, Lovely Christmas," sung to the tune of "Holy Night." The youngest member of the family approaches the tree first.

In Denmark, the *Nisse* takes the place of Santa Claus. He is actually a much smaller creature than Santa Claus, and is often referred to as an elf or a sprite. For the last hundred years, the *Nisser* (plural for *Nisse*) have attached themselves to Danish homes. Today the *Nisse* is the lone surviving representative of the many supernatural beings who played a part in the Danish Yuletide of bygone days. These gnomelike creatures are given to all sorts of mischief—even as children are at Halloween—but, on the whole, they are good little sprites.

On the farm, they keep a friendly eye on cows and horses in the barn and on other domestic animals as well, in town and country. They frequently appear on Danish Christmas cards, often in the company of the house cat. According to old Danish folk belief, they actually marry and have children. The old *Nisse* of the family has a long white beard like Santa's, and all, both young and old, wear red caps. Among other things, they remind folk to pour milk in a saucer for the cat, and it is customary to put a plate of rice porridge outside the kitchen door on Christmas Eve for the *Nisse*. The plate is always licked clean by morning. Only unimaginative souls would think of saying that the cat must have eaten the porridge!

England

Lamp-lighters and bell-ringers, toy-sellers and carol-singers—all are quaint reminders of the day when a coach-and-four, amid the blare of trumpets, pulled up in front of an English inn or a great house to celebrate Christmas. Tall hats and greatcoats, muffs and mufflers, footwarmers and gaiters were quickly disposed of as the guests hastened toward their mugs of Christmas cheer. The pipers would soon appear to play the first of the quadrilles, "Speed the Plough" or "Bernie Bough." This was a merry time, indeed. Wassailing and feasting, playing games galore, and participating in an assortment of pantomimes, puppet shows, and parties—all made the holiday season in both town and country one long, mad, merry revel from Christmas Eve to Twelfth Night.

Washington Irving and Charles Dickens were the chief historians of the English Christmas. Their heartwarming stories, rich in detail and description, evoked a nostalgic ring still heard today. They captured the "old-fashioned Christmas" and portrayed it with enduring enchantment. As a result, citizens of the British Isles, of North America (and, for that matter, of a large part of the civilized world), have long cherished this romantic concept of Christmas as an ideal to be perpetuated and nurtured. For more than a century these age-old traditions, vividly depicted in a glowing and fanciful manner on greeting cards, have preserved this nostalgic image of Christmas. In Victorian days, holiday greetings blossomed like flowers and bespoke their message in tender sentiment printed in brilliant color. Thus, for generations, inspired by these two romanticists and a host of other long-forgotten chroniclers, illustrators have used their talents lavishly, literally overwhelming us with the warmth and the sentiment of the season—a feeling so welcome at the cold time of the year that it has become part and parcel of the holiday season.

In like manner, bringing in the Yule log, serving up the boar's head, hanging the mistletoe, tolling the Devil's knell, and burning the ashen faggot are rites linked with ancient ceremonial aspects of the English Christmas now seldom practiced. Yet, they are still observed in remote villages of this ancient land, where even the smallest hamlet clings tenaciously to its hallowed traditions. Time has changed some of these customs and consecrated others.

33

Not just one shop, but the whole of London's Regent Street is dressed in a fabulous mantle of colored, sparkling lights and trimmings at Christmas time. Stars and crescents glitter in the sky high above the double-decker buses; Christmas trees are aflame with light; all is fairyland. *Courtesy British Travel Association.*

As night falls on Christmas Eve at the Tower of London, a group of choir boys tour the towers and residences within the mighty walls of this ancient fort. Young voices echo around the weathered stone, dispelling any thoughts of headless figures wandering away from the block. Just in case, though, these Beefeaters act as escort. *Courtesy British Travel Association.*

"This is the one for me!" The Lowther Arcade has disappeared and its place as a Christmas attraction has been taken by the great stores which, in their festive dress, are almost as good as fairyland. Especially when someone asks you to choose the doll (or the rabbit) you like best. *Courtesy British Travel Association.*

At Christmas time the centerpiece of London's public decorations is Trafalger Square, where, each year since 1947, a large Christmas tree is erected beside Nelson's Column and the floodlit fountains. The tree is an annual gift to Londoners from the people of Oslo, Norway. *Courtesy British Travel Association.*

During the past three hundred years, the festive season in England which once lasted twelve days or more has been shortened considerably. Many of the old folkways have lost their significance because of changes in the mode and manner of living and are now practically forgotten. They live only in books or in the conversations of those who enjoy reminiscence and the delights of the past. On the other hand, traditions have a way of being modified, adapted, and reinterpreted to serve the needs of a changing world as original meanings give way to new outlooks and attitudes. Thus, timeworn beliefs sometimes emerge in new guise.

In England, as everywhere in the world where Christmas is observed, children revel in the season of joy and good will. It is their time of greatest joy, since they have what Leslie Daiken describes as "a special share in the glory that radiates from Bethlehem. They are, for a time, privileged beings, entitled to a place of honor in the festivities; and so it is that at the centre of our Christmas celebrations is not only a Child but all childhood. That, perhaps, is why Christmas never seems to change, for children themselves do not want change; they prefer the familiar things, and what they liked a hundred years ago they still like today." The only difference is that the toys are more wonderful each year, as dolls become more lifelike in appearance and the latest space toys offer new diversion for the boys.

The toys are distributed on Christmas afternoon rather than on the previous evening, as is the way in many parts of Europe. Father Christmas is another name for Santa Claus or St. Nicholas in Britain. Children write letters to him listing their wants and desires and sometimes toss them into the back of the fireplace. If the message is carried up the chimney by the draft, the sender is assured of having his requests fulfilled; but, if it is consumed in the flames, another try is made to assure proper delivery of the magic message. This is apparently a more direct way of reaching Father Christmas than depending on the postman.

Stockings are hung to receive the hoped-for gifts since it is related that, one Christmas Eve, St. Nicholas accidentally dropped some gold coins down one of the tricky chimneys through which he was making his way. Ordinarily, they would have dropped into the grate, but instead they fell into a stocking left by the fireside to dry. Ever since that time the generous giver of gifts is expected to fill every stocking which has been set out in anticipation of his arrival.

On both sides of the Atlantic, the excitement and extra-special delight that come from visiting toy shops is something not easily described. And the pleasurable sensations are not limited to youngsters. Leslie Daiken sounds a poignant note as he recalls memories of those unforgettable days when it was "a great treat for London boys and girls to be taken to the Lowther Arcade in the Strand—a great covered market where a breath-taking variety of toys was displayed on the stalls. But, though the Arcade has disappeared, its place has been filled by other delights which are perhaps even better—the Christmas toy displays in the great stores, with their magic caves and fairy grottoes, which bring that glow of wonderment into a child's eyes that is the reward of every parent."

The toy peddlers who appear from nowhere at Christmas with their animated rabbits, walking dolls, and alarmingly lifelike snakes hark back to the days of

35

the great fairs, circus time, and summer festivals. Their antics and their wares are as eye-catching as ever, and the simple mechanism that made Jack-in-the-box the delight of children in Victorian days is the same device that now gives twentieth-century gewgaws their appeal and their magic.

Bringing in the Yule log—a tradition which has been highly romanticized—is an ancient folkway that has practically disappeared. Few fireplaces today are large enough to accommodate the enormous log that was once used—enormous because it was expected to last from Christmas Eve until Epiphany. In the days of the Vikings, who introduced the practice to England, the log was burned in honor of the god Thor, but over the centuries Britain and other countries adapted the practice to the observance of Christmas. It was customary to drag in a carefully selected log from the nearby forest and ceremoniously place it on the massive hearth. A burst of song welcomed its arrival on Christmas Eve, which was spent, by masters and servants alike, feasting in front of the fire. The whole scene was one of color and anticipation of the great Christmas Day banquets. Any fragments left from one year's Yule log were carefully saved to be used for kindling the next year.

The boar's head ceremony, immortalized by Washington Irving and Dickens, is one of England's feudal customs still cherished at Queen's College, Oxford. Each year a boar's head, gaily festooned with pennants, bay, holly, and rosemary, becrowned and with an orange in its mouth, is borne into the brightly decorated hall, where it is the centerpiece of a rite which has been observed for centuries. To the provost, fellows, and dons of the College assembled in the hall with their guests, the arrival of the elaborately garnished head is heralded with singing by the college choir and a fanfare of trumpets. Carried head-high through the hall on a huge silver dish, the boar's head is lowered onto the provost's table as the choir sings the last notes of a familiar carol. The provost then removes the ornaments and embellishments one by one from the head and presents them to the choir boys and the visitors. To the soloist of the year goes the orange from the boar's mouth.

As James Street reminds us, "Boars' heads have been featured in banquets for hundreds of years, especially in the north of England. There it is believed to be a survival of an old Norse custom in which a boar was sacrificed at Yuletide feasts in honour of Freyr, the Scandinavian god of peace and plenty. The Queen's College ceremony has its own particular tradition. It is said that in the early days of the college a student was walking in the neighbouring forest of Shotover, engrossed in a volume of Aristotle, when a wild boar charged him. With great presence of mind, the student rammed the book down the boar's throat and choked it."

Another old Christmas custom is observed every year in the Yorkshire borough of Dewsbury. Known as "Tolling the Devil's Knell," this rite has been carried on for seven hundred years, with only a short break in continuity during the war years, when bell-ringing was forbidden for security reasons. Each year, on Christmas Eve, a team of bell-ringers tolls the tenor bell of the parish church—once for every year since the birth of Christ. The final stroke is timed to ring exactly at the hour of midnight. Legend says that the practice began in the thirteenth century when a local baron, as penance for killing one of his

36

servants, gave a bell to the church and ordered that it be rung each Christmas Eve to remind him of his crime. For many years the good people of Dewsbury believed that the tolling of the bell would keep the Devil away from their parish for the next twelve months.

Throughout England, there are many ceremonies connected with the ringing of bells, steeped in tradition, that have fascinating associations with this season of joy. A very ancient custom observed every Christmas Eve at Dunster, in Somerset, is the burning of the ashen faggot. This custom is believed to be more than a thousand years old. Before entering the fray in the battles in Wessex in 878, the West Saxon warriors built fires of ash branches to warm themselves at night. They discovered that ash was the only fuel that would burn when green. The worthy men and women of Dunster still continue burning the faggot, though it is now a prelude to nothing more fierce than a battle for partners at a dance.

Gypsy tribes in various parts of Europe have a similar ceremony which they observe with elaborate ritual. They cherish an old belief shared in many parts of the Old World that the Christ Child was first bathed and dressed by a fire made of wood from the ash tree.

Christmas mummers perform in the streets and the inns of some towns and villages in the West Country with the same enthusiasm as they did centuries ago. At Eynsham, Broadway, and Chipping Campden, in the Cotswold country, these mummers present a masque depicting two men fighting and the vanquished one being raised from the dead by a doctor—the local traditional version of death and resurrection. In previous centuries, this type of performance was frowned upon by church and civil authority alike. The mummers at Longparish and Overton in Hampshire, arrayed like grotesque birds with monstrous headdresses, tour the village singing carols. Similar demonstrations of this sort are carried on in the mountains of Austria, in Provence, and by Indian tribes in Peru.

Long ago, the English poets made famous the quaint and ancient practice of decking the halls with holly, ivy, and other greens to dispel the gloominess of the dark days of winter. Hanging mistletoe, also a relic from the mists of antiquity, stemming from the Druid ceremonials, is among the oldest of all English holiday customs. Hanging ale garlands outside inns "to signify that good ale awaits within has long been regarded as a simple expression of festivity, hospitality and good fellowship" associated with English inns. Some families light their windows with strings of electric lights and doors are adorned with bunches of greens and swags, but using wreaths for doorway decoration is not so popular in England as in North America.

The kissing bunch suspended from the ceiling—a circlet of greens made of hoops studded with candles and embellished with apples—was originally a simplified kind of manger setting complete with wax figures of the Holy Family. In many ways, it was the forerunner of the Christmas tree since it also served as a safe place to store small gifts prior to Christmas, when they were poked out with sticks by the eager children. The chief ornament of the kissing bunch is always a cluster of mistletoe and the ceremony surrounding it today is universally popular with all ages. As Katharine Van Etten Lyford has expressed it in *The Kissing Bunch Still Hangs High:* "A wonderful contraption, that Christmas kissing bunch! Beneath it boy met girl with explosive results for custom de-

37

manded that when a Man catch his Woman he may kiss until her ears crack or she will be disappointed, if she is a Woman of any Spirit."

No country in Europe has more effectively introduced its cherished Christmas customs to other lands that Germany, whose Christmas-keeping burghers transported their beloved symbol, the decorated evergreen tree, all over Europe and America in the nineteenth century. They endowed it with a kind of missionary zeal, and everyone who saw the Christmas tree learned to love it and made it a part of his own Christmas.

So it was in England that Prince Albert sought to delight Queen Victoria and the royal family in 1841. To be sure, the Christmas tree was not entirely new at the time, for Victoria had known about it as a small child, but after 1841 this gaily decked evergreen symbol became the vogue almost immediately. Tinsel and glittering ornaments, together with fruit, nuts, candy and cookies, trinkets and notions of a practical nature, knitted and crocheted, are still the stuff that makes a glamorous setting for the toys that bedeck the jeweled trees of Christmas.

Each year since World War II, the people of Oslo, Norway, have sent to London a huge native spruce which is set up, lighted and decorated, with great ceremony in Trafalgar Square. It serves as a token of Norway's appreciation for Great Britain's cooperation during the war and adds another ever-green link to the chain of tradition which ornaments the symbolic tree in many lands.

In every English household, the fresh and pungent aromas that come from the kitchen augur well for a joyous holiday long before December 25th. Wonderful tales have been written and equally wonderful drawings have been made of the ritual surrounding the making and serving of plum pudding, which probably acquired its name from the dried plums formerly used as ingredients. From the time of assembling the makings to the mixing and stirring, cooking, and final serving of this tasty dish is a long stretch—a matter of weeks. Puddings are sometimes made in quantity and kept in the larder for several years. Wishes are made while the pudding is stirred, and all the family may have a hand in it if they choose. It is an old-time practice to wrap coins or trinkets (especially for the children) and to put them in the pudding as harbingers of good luck to their finders. Decorated with holly and brought to the table surrounded by a halo of flaming brandy, the pudding is the crowning glory of the Christmas dinner, and few traditions relating to good eating are enjoyed more generally beyond the shores of England than plum pudding.

Small mince pies, the size of tarts, are popular as treats for the carol singers who appear on Christmas Eve and during the holidays, and for visitors as well. Since it has been a long-cherished notion that the twelve days of Christmas represent the twelve months of the year, everyone is eager to eat at least twelve pies to assure an entire year of good fortune. A roll made with bits of sausage rolled in a flaky crust is another seasonal delicacy.

Christmas cake, often made as early as September, calls for ample amounts of citron, marzipan, many kinds of candied peel—orange, lemon, grapefruit—and other ingredients, the whole topped off with brandy. The result is a rich concoction that keeps well for a long time, covered with almond paste and a handsome sugar frosting, prettily decorated. Usually the first sampling is at teatime on Christmas Day.

38

Christmas is the time for carols. The high-pitched trebles of the young choristers blend with the resonant basses of the men to make a memorable sound. *Courtesy British Travel Association.*

It has been said that Charles Dickens invented Christmas—the English Christmas, anyway. Here members of the Blackheath Male Voice Choir set out on an evening's caroling. They are dressed in the costume of the Dickens period. And what better starting-place than the Old Curiosity Shop in London, immortalized by the great writer! *Courtesy British Travel Association.*

Dinner on Christmas Day features turkey with chestnut stuffing or served with sausage and bacon rings. Brussels sprouts and cauliflower are almost certain to be on the menu.

Throughout the Old World, and in the Americas as well, the singing of carols is a practice that has been enjoyed for hundreds of years. Carols—or noëls, as originally written—were cries of joy uttered at Christmas. The term "carol" also refers to a kind of round dance accompanied by gay songs, once popular. Some of the most beautiful of these musical compositions date from the time of Francis of Assisi in the thirteenth century. As they became more popular and more highly secularized, the themes of some of the carols drifted away from the religious aspects of Christmas. Nevertheless, the heritage of every nation is rich in these delightful musical rhymes, full of tenderness, compassion, wonder, and joy. Carols are sung at church services on Christmas Eve, again on Christmas Day, and whenever the occasion arises during the season.

Groups of carolers, formerly referred to as "waits," create a spirit of glee and playfulness as they sing, first with reverence, and then change to the lighter side of the holiday season. The term "waits" was formerly linked with the hautboy or oboe, an instrument popular with roving groups of carolers in bygone days. These Christmas entertainers traveled about at night and they were granted licenses to perform. Wind instruments were popular among them. The "buskers" seen today on the streets of London and other English cities at Christmas, performing for all who pass by with the hope of earning a few pence, are their lineal descendants. Appearing at twilight, full-throated, and sometimes carrying instruments for accompaniment, they never fail to lift the hearts of their listeners. And it is difficult to believe that anyone could join a group who did not love to sing!

Boxing Day, the first weekday after Christmas, a kind of prolongation of Christmas Day, is so-called from the practice of giving boxes of food, gifts, and money to tenants, tradesmen, and those who render service in any way. During the sixteenth century, Boxing Day was of special interest to the English court. It is said that Queen Elizabeth depended heavily on her subjects for annual gifts of petticoats, furs, and other items to replenish her wardrobe. She is believed to be the first woman to have received a pair of silk stockings at Christmas. Boxing Day also bids well for the roving troupes of carol singers, groups of youngsters, and the unfortunates of the community.

Actually, this custom can be traced back to pagan times. In its present-day observance, however, such post-Christmas activities as the opening of the Pantomime are important. Such beloved children's classics as Cinderella, Puss in Boots, Jack and the Bean Stalk, Aladdin, and other old favorites are presented in a most elaborate manner for the delight of the younger generation. Punch and Judy still survive.

In Provence, an entire family may devote its talents to making *santons*.

All the animals come to adore the Christ Child. Some of these *santons* are less than half an inch high.

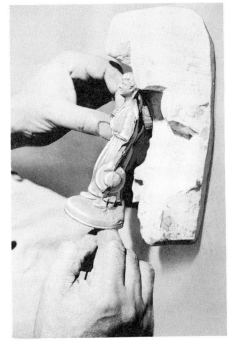

An unfinished *santon* ready to be removed from its mold.

France

As with many nations in the Old World, Christmas in France is linked with a series of notable historical events. However, the observance of the Christ Child's birthday has never been as important a national holiday as New Year's Day. Customs vary in different parts of the country, colored by the influence of adjoining nations and by folkways introduced from a variety of cultures: Greek, Roman, and Oriental. Roman domination brought a wealth of holiday customs which originated in the Orient. The *farandole,* a folk dance popular in Provence and adjoining regions at Christmas and on other holidays, can be traced to Greece. The Yule log, wassailing the fruit trees, the ceremony of going to meet the Wise Men on Epiphany Eve, the dispersal of gifts from the Urn of Fate, and many other practices discussed in detail elsewhere in this book were all adapted from neighboring countries.

Probably the first Christmas celebration held in France was at Rheims in 496, when Clovis and three thousand of his warriors were baptized. It is recorded that Bishop Remi had chosen the day of the Nativity purposely for this ceremony. On Christmas Day in the year 800, Charlemagne was "crowned by God the Great and Pacific Emperor" under the auspices of Pope Leo III. Three centuries later, Godefroy de Bouillon's successor, his brother Baudouin, was crowned in the basilica of Saint Marie of Bethlehem. Later still, King Jean-le-Bon founded the Order of the Star in honor of the Mater which remained in existence until 1352. In 1389, the crowds welcomed Queen Isabeau of Bavaria with the joyous cry, "Noël! Noël!"

Gradually Christmas became a religious and secular celebration, and, until the end of the Middle Ages, the observance of the great day vied with that of New Year's Day. Today, Christmas in France is essentially a family holiday, a religious celebration, and an occasion for merrymaking for the children. New Year's Day, on the other hand, is more strictly an adult festival, when gifts are exchanged and social calls are made.

The Christmas tree has never been as popular in France as it is in many European countries, despite the fact that it has been known there for more than a century. "That pretty German toy," as Dickens called it, has always been something of a novelty cherished principally by foreigners, but in recent years the symbolic tree and the traditions linked with it have been more widely adopted in some regions of France. Decorated shopwindows and department stores are seen everywhere. Animated figures of the storybook world whose antics are a perpetual source of delight to all ages are featured in shopwindows throughout Paris.

In every part of France, churches and cathedrals are magnificently lighted for the three midnight Masses customarily celebrated. The joyful melodies of carols, bells, and carillons lift the hearts of all as they gather to pay homage to the Christ Child. Most churches have elaborate *crèches,* many of which are cherished for their great beauty and their antiquity. Formerly, in certain regions, a real infant was placed on the hay of the *crèche* during the Mass, but this custom, so beloved by the peasants, is no longer observed.

The *Santon* Fair at Marseilles. *Santons* were sold at fairs here and at Aix as early as 1803, continuing the tradition of the fair that was in progress in Bethlehem when the Christ Child was born. *Courtesy Hélène P. Carter.*

Wassailing the fruit trees at Christmas is an ancient rite that was commonly observed in practically every country in Europe. Scattering ashes from the Yule Log was another practice. Both customs were associated with the belief that the trees would thereby yield more abundantly.

When the family returns home after midnight Mass, the repast or late supper served is known as *le réveillon*. Every region has its favorite dishes. In Alsace, the goose is brought in on a platter and given the place of honor on the table. The Bretons serve buckwheat cakes with sour cream, while turkey and chestnuts are favored in Burgundy. The favorite dishes of Paris and the Ile-de-France region are oysters, *foie gras,* and the traditional cake in the form of a Yule log, which reminds one of the *bûche de Noël* (Yule log) that used to be burned on the hearth on Christmas Eve. Wines, an assortment of fruit, and sweets are included.

In Paris, Christmas is more worldly and is observed in a much more sophisticated manner than among the countryfolk. For many Parisiens, the religious aspects and the traditional significance of the festival have become overshadowed by dancing and dining in style at the various restaurants and cafés.

Before going to bed, children put their shoes by the fireside expecting a gift from *le père Noël* or *le petit Jesus.* Formerly, peasants' wooden shoes, called *sabots,* were very popular at Christmastime, but today shoes of any kind are set before the fireplace or around the tree in some sections. However, the *sabots* are not forgotten since the pastry shops make chocolate wooden shoes filled with candies which still serve as reminders of the old custom.

In France, as everywhere in Europe, Christmas carols (*noëls* or *nouvés,* as they are called) evolved from the miracle and mystery plays of the Middle Ages. They have been aptly described as the "*crèche* created into song." Most of these *noëls* are purely imaginative, having been inspired by the apocryphal scriptures and colored by the fascinating childlike legends that spring from the minds of people who are close to the soil. In most instances, the composers were not trained musicians with university backgrounds: by nature they were troubadours while by occupation they were carpenters, wood-sellers, and tradesmen of various sorts. These "simple-hearted singers of Bethlehem," reaching into the lives of the people, frequently used the musical scores of popular songs and dances to make their poetic phrases appealing. And they imparted to their simple compositions a feeling of tenderness and devotion enhanced by a spirit of adoration that was intensely human.

When the utter poverty of the Virgin stirred the pity of the noëlist, he would tell of all the gifts that the new mother and her Child were to receive. The shepherdesses brought woolen cloth to swaddle the infant Jesus, a binder, a skein, pieces of linen, a cap and a bonnet, as well as a pine-wood case full of clothes. We hear the chattering around the manger: "Pass me the foot warmer (*chauferette*), quick. There. Warm up His clothes, Guilaumette."

As fashions changed, so too did the songs of Christmas. The eighteenth century brought in the element of burlesque and the lively music of the gavotte and the minuet, followed in later decades by carols of a rather pompous character. Nonetheless, the great treasury of French carols is exceedingly rich and varied, with charming pieces to suit every taste.

During the fourteenth and the fifteenth centuries, the heyday of the miracle and mystery plays, Biblical scenes connected with the story of Christ's birth were especially popular. They were presented with simple stage settings, but the action was so lively and so realistic that the message conveyed left a deep im-

44

print on the minds of the audience. Today, many of these Christmas plays, full of awe and wonder, are still enjoyed as they were long ago. Among them is "Mystères de la Nativité," written by Marguerite, queen of Navarre, at the beginning of the sixteenth century.

Then, too, puppet shows have continued to hold their appeal for both young and old. They are given every year at Christmas, principally in Paris and in Lyons, and bring back memories of that era prior to the movies when spirited peep shows were commonplace at all sorts of gatherings. One of the well-known Christmas puppet plays written by de Marynbourg, called "Bethlehem 1933," is considered a masterpiece of popular art.

Every region of France is rich in traditional legends and folkways associated with Christmas. In Provence, the great holiday is celebrated with much community spirit and joy. In towns like Les Baux, shepherds offer a lamb to the priest at the end of the midnight Mass on Christmas Eve. The *réveillon* is held in the snowy mountains or a songfest precedes the midnight Mass. In the small village of Solliesville, the whole population gathers in order to take bread. Twelve children are selected, and each one receives an obol of bread, meat, and candies as a symbol of the apostles. Then supper is offered to the important townsmen and their guests. During the Mass, the characters of the manger scene are portrayed by people from the village.

The magic of Christmas is the magic of the Orient. During the Middle Ages, minstrels wandered through villages and towns, telling of "Merveilles qui advinrent en la Sainte Nuit," the story of the flight into Egypt, or the legend of the sower who, when asked which way the Holy Family had gone, deceived King Herod. Nearly all the legends told around the fire on Christmas Eve have been forgotten, but some of them have been preserved as fairy tales. Such a story is that of the dancers condemned to dance throughout the year because their movements had distracted a priest's thoughts during midnight Mass on Christmas Eve. Another such tale is that of the pathetic and charming match-seller who, sitting in the snow on the sidewalk because she was homeless, struck all her matches in order to imagine Christmas in a house. Since Christmas is the time of miracles, at the striking of the last match, the little girl was conveyed to Paradise by shining angels.

In Alsace, it used to be the custom to set up a *mai* in the public square for New Year's Day. This age-old tradition may well have been a forerunner of the community Christmas tree, so popular in North America today. Usually the tree, its lower limbs stripped, was erected near a fountain. The term *mai* refers not to the month of the calendar year, as might be assumed, but rather means "to decorate" or "to adorn." Ribbons, decorated eggshells, dolls, and usually a figure of a shepherd or a man beating his wife were hung on the tree, which was put in place on New Year's Eve. On the following day, the girls of the village who set it up assembled for a dance and the boys were allowed to take part only when the girls gave them permission. It is interesting that this tree was allowed to remain standing throughout the year as a symbol of protection for the maidens who put it there.

In Provence, the Christmas *crèche* has a unique kind of charm. The making of the tiny clay figures, known as *santons,* and the setting of the *crèche* itself are a rare combination of childlike naïveté and craftsmanship animated by simple faith and warm devotion. For a century and a half, village craftsmen and their families have devoted their spare hours throughout the year to the fashioning of the "little saints," and these are sold at the great Christmas fairs held each year early in December at Marseilles and at Aix.

About 1800, a group of Italian peddlers from Naples appeared in the streets of Marseilles selling small religious figures made of brightly colored plaster. These were known as *santi belli,* and included the Virgin Mary, various saints, bishops, and the pope. Attracted by the appeal which these brightly colored images had for the local populace, artisans and craftsmen began to make similar figures of the common clay used for pottery.

At about this time, a macaroni-maker named Antoine Maurel wrote a delightful fantasy—a kind of mystery play featuring the Nativity—which he called "Pastorale." It dramatized the story of how the shepherds learned of the Messiah's birth on that first Christmas Eve in Bethlehem and led to the holy stable the entire village, including other shepherds whom they met and peasants whom they awakened—to bring greetings and gifts to the Christ Child. This play so delighted the people that the *santon* makers modeled shepherds in many poses to put in the little Christmas cribs which were becoming popular for home use in Provence. The various actors in the play served as models for the *santon* makers, and these were added to the figures to be used in the little Christmas *crèches.* These included the mayor; an old man named Jourdan with his lantern; Margarido, the village gossip, with her umbrella, sometimes shown walking and sometimes on a donkey; simple-minded Bartoumieu, with his *fougasse* cake; Giget and his codfish; and a number of other local characters.

The actors of the "Pastorale," though depicting an event that happened at the beginning of the Christian era, were dressed in the fashions of the early nineteenth century, just as the Romans and Greeks in Racine's classical tragedies wore the wigs and the costumes of the time of Louis XIV. The same convention was followed by the *santon* makers. These figures were habited not only according to their period but also according to their locality. They are country people from the villages of Aubagne, Roquevain, Auriol, and Aix. They include the peasant in his blue smock, with a garland of silver-skinned onions around his neck; the peasant's wife, with an enormous basket of vegetables and a couple of chickens; and the woman with a green and yellow pottery jug.

As time went on, each *santon* maker developed his own series of characters, who represented the peasants and the artisans of his particular village. These were grouped with their gifts around the Holy Family, and each had a story to tell. Here were the knife grinder, the local judge, the washerwoman, the gypsy, the thief, the drummer boy, the blind man, the town crier, the faggot woman, the herb gatherer, and so forth.

46

The gardener carries flowers in one hand and a watering can in the other. His cotton trousers, yellow shirt without tie, open waistcoat, and pointed straw hat are those of most countryside gardeners. The hunter has exactly that triumphant look worn by all the hunters you meet in Provence during the hunting season. He has his dog with him on a leash and carries the hare he has killed as proudly as a king wears his crown.

Many of the *santons* surprise us by the harmonious richness of their costumes. Here is old Jourdan with a yellow polka dot waistcoat and a red tie knotted under his high collar. Children—and their parents, too—never tire of admiring his breeches, his leggings, his blue-and-white striped bonnet.

It is especially interesting to notice how the *santons* have followed the changes that have taken place in both home and public life in Provence in the last century and a half. Those made in the early 1800's were dressed in the style of their day. As styles changed in the world, so they changed in the *santons*, which reflect the world. When it became customary for men to ride horseback through the lowlands taking care of their cattle, a new popular figure appeared, similar to our Western cowboy. Thus, in the Provence of today, the tradition of the *santons* maintains its old appeal to the children in being up-to-date and close to reality.

Many people who have studied the subject of European Christmas *crèches* are convinced that Marseilles excels all other important centers of production, such as Bavaria, the Tyrol, and southern Italy.

It is customary—and, in fact, traditional—to attribute the origin, or at least the popularization, of the Christmas crib (*crèche*) to St. Francis of Assisi, for it was he who made the Christmas crib come to life in a very real way on that memorable Christmas Eve in the Umbrian Hills in the year 1223. An old tradition in Provence has it that Pope John XXII, the second of the Avignon popes, brought the custom of the Christmas crib to Provence in or about the year 1316. After that time, elaborate cribs with handsomely dressed dolls were made for cathedrals and churches throughout the south of France.

Another thread in the tapestry is the growth of miracle and mystery plays in France, England, Germany, and Italy. Later, the development in France of automatic toys, or automatons, made the Christmas crib popular when it was presented in the form of a peep show, with many lively personalities adding to the gaiety and the spirit of the Nativity scene.

In true peasant fashion, the *santonniers* of Provence have captured the spirit of Bethlehem and have dramatized their devotion and joy in a way that is warm, spontaneous, and touchingly personal. In the words of Marcel Provence, "the man who makes a *santon* plays God the Father, and like Him, fashions a man from clay."

47

Germany

Germany, often referred to as the country best known for "Christmas keeping," long ago made the Christmas tree its national symbol of the season, and through their love for and their loyalty to their own traditions and customs the German people have literally spread its use all across the world.

In the Middle Ages, it was customary to hold a special observance of the feast day of Adam and Eve on December 24th. The day was a festive one, during which plays were presented dramatizing the lives of the first dwellers in the Garden of Eden. Among the props used on the stage was an evergreen tree decorated with apples, placed there to remind the audience of the Fall of Man. The plays were greatly expanded over the years and their popularity grew as they became more worldly in action, humor, and realism. Finally, the religious significance of the miracle and mystery plays became greatly overshadowed by coarseness of speech and horseplay introduced as humor. When these folk dramas finally were abandoned by the Church, the German peasants set up evergreen trees in their homes and decorated them with apples.

On Christmas Eve, it was also the custom to light a group of candles arranged in a candlestand, often of pyramidal design, called a "lightstock." This tradition, which signified Christ as the Light of the World, was a most appropriate symbol for Christmas Eve. Gradually, the candles from the lightstock were transferred to the evergreen decked with apples. Later, thin cookies were added which served as symbols of the sweets of the Redemption, since they were round in form like the Sacred Host. In addition to their symbolic significance, the apples, the candles, and the cookies created highly decorative effects on the tree. This, in brief, is the origin of the Christmas tree in Christian folk tradition. From this beginning, rich in symbolism, the festive tree has become a world-wide symbol, and nowhere beyond the borders of Germany is it more popular than in North America.

From Germany, a nation steeped in Christmas lore, all the world has been the recipient of the heritage of Christmas decorations, particularly the colorful blown-glass baubles in a variety of shapes (substitutes for the apples), ornate paper cornucopias, fancy cutouts, angels in endless variety, and all those glorious and brilliant tinsel ornaments so dear to the hearts of children—and grown-ups too. However, since World War II, nearly all the colored Christmas balls used in the United States have been produced by one of our own leading glass manufacturers.

In the Victorian era, when the Christmas tree took root in the United States, Henry Van Dyke wrote *The First Christmas Tree,* which records one of the oldest German legends relating to its origin. This charming narrative tells how St. Boniface, earlier known as Wynfred, brought Christianity to Germany. Like many of the early missionaries who went into strange lands to preach the Gospel, his life was one of hardship and privation. His early work among the German people brought him recognition from Pope Gregory II at Rome, but he returned to his adopted country to find that the eldest son of the Chieftain Gundhar was to be sacrificed to the gods on Christmas Eve. A giant oak, sacred to their patron Thor, was to be the scene of the sacrifice. Boniface wished to destroy this pagan symbol if only to prove that the pagan deity was powerless. After one stroke with the ax, a wind toppled the mighty oak. The assembled throng was awed by what happened and asked Boniface for the word of God. Pointing to an evergreen growing nearby, he replied:

"This is the word, and this is the counsel. Not a drop of blood shall fall tonight, for this is the birth-night of the Saint Christ, Son of the All-Father and Saviour of the world. This little tree, a young child of the forest, shall be a home tree tonight. It is the wood of peace, for your houses are built of fir. It is the sign of endless life, for its branches are ever green. See how it points toward Heaven! Let this be called the tree of the Christ Child; gather about it, not in the wild woods but in your homes; there it will shelter no deeds of blood, but loving gifts and lights of kindness."

The wood of the fallen oak was used to build a little monastery and a church dedicated to St. Peter. The fir tree was cut and taken to Gundhar's great hall, where it was set up for the observance of Christmas. This, according to a beloved German legend, was the first Christmas tree.

Another deeply rooted story about the origin of the Christmas tree, widely told since the days of the Reformation, refers to Martin Luther. After walking one Christmas Eve under the cold December sky which was illumined by countless stars, he returned home and set up a tree for the delight of his wife and children. Lighting the little evergreen he had carried from the nearby woods with great numbers of candles, he used this glowing symbol to tell his children the true meaning of the Christ Child, the Light of the World, whose birth had so gloriously brightened the sky on that first Christmas Eve. Since there is no documented record for this story, it has been relegated to the realm of tradition, but it could well have happened; in fact, it might well have transpired even though not recorded. Whatever the facts, like so many old traditions the story lives on and adds color, luster, and meaning to the ever-growing garland of Christmas-

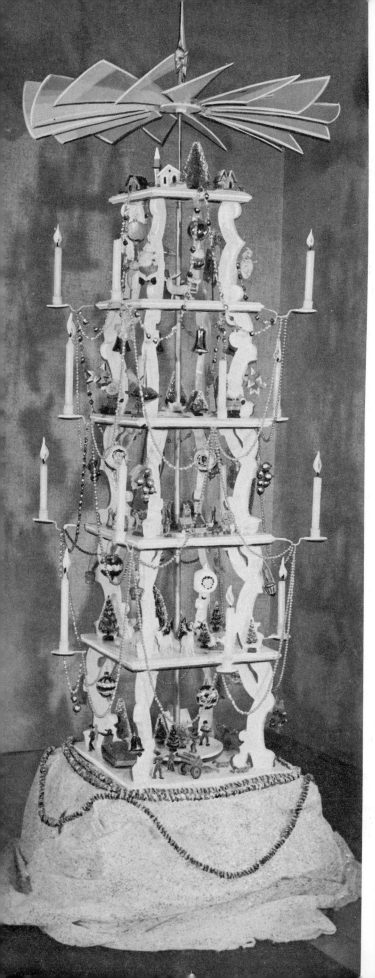

Madonna and Child in the German tradition.

A revolving pyramid typical of the permanent types of Christmas trees popular in Central Europe two centuries ago. *Courtesy Zaharis.*

Cradle-rocking was a part of Christmas observance in Germany in bygone days in which the clergy and the altar boys took part.

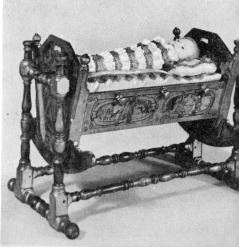

tree lore. Actually, the Christmas tree had been familiar to the German people long before the time of Martin Luther.

"At Christmas, fir trees are set up in the rooms at Strasbourg and hung with roses cut from paper of many colors, apples, wafers, spangle-gold, sugar, etc. It is customary to surround it with a square frame . . . and in front . . ." The rest of the account unfortunately has been lost. This widely quoted reference, dated 1603, is the first authentic written record of an actual Christmas tree as we know it today. An earlier printed record, dated 1521, makes mention of the tree in German Alsace. However, there is no mention of lights in this brief reference, nor in the Strasbourg account. As early as 1755, a regulation pertaining to the forests of Salzburg forbade the taking of small evergreen trees or bushes from the forests. This would indicate that the Christmas tree was becoming a popular institution even then.

Pagan influences are evident in the observance of Christmas everywhere in the Old World. In Germany, the Roman conquest left its mark, and the mingling of a number of ancient beliefs which were adapted by the early Christians has resulted in a plethora of colorful customs whose origin is easily traced back to the time of Caesar. Naturally, the ceremonies connected with the winter solstice, which embraced the Yule god Thor and the goddess Hertha, patroness of the home, have left their imprint. Both inspired the impulse of gift-bringing as tribute. Thus, the St. Nicholas tradition which developed in the early centuries of the Christian era is easy to explain. In like manner, the Yule tree arose from a pagan custom which required an evergreen to be set up indoors or near the entrance to the house to dispel the gloom of winter and to remind the populace that the ever-green branches signified the continuing cycle of the seasons.

Inherent skill in wood carving and the making of figures from a variety of materials gave impetus to the fashion for Christmas cribs among the German peasants. Folk beliefs, wrapped in tender concern for the welfare of the Christ Child and the creature comforts due him as King of the World, resulted in such unusual practices as cradle-rocking in the churches at Christmas. It was an old custom to rock a cradle containing an image of the Christ Child with the priest and the altar boys participating as they danced about singing carols.

Nearly every nation in the world has its store of customs and traditions associated with Christmas, but few can surpass the all-embracing scope of the German folkways, for they express every phase of the symbolic season. In every part of the German nation, the citizenry cherish age-old beliefs, traditional foods, ancient ceremonials and symbolism, music and verse, that are the very earmarks of the festive season. The wonderful world of toyland and the fanciful realm of baubles and tinsel are also of German origin. The country people, particularly, had a way of perpetuating and keeping green their beloved traditions. Everywhere they went, as they migrated from the homeland, they carried with them memories of Christmas as they had known and loved it and with all the enthusiasm of zealots they made their heartfelt sentiments come alive in their new homes.

Preparing for the festive season has always meant something special in every part of Germany. The toy makers looked upon Christmas as a year-long time of getting ready, for they contributed the playthings that made the children of

51

A nineteenth-century German Christmas market.

The spirit of German Christmas, with its emphasis on home festivities, has left its imprint the world over.

the world happy. The makers of baubles and tinsel also spent months at their crafts, making the products which were shipped around the globe.

Hanging a wreath of greens bearing four candles, one to be lighted on each Sunday of Advent (the four-week period of preparation for Christmas), represents but one of many customs passed down for centuries in German culture. Making cookies and cakes, the holiday mood of the Christmas market, the tradition of the tree and the Christmas crib, and a dozen other episodes of family participation have made of German Christmas a truly extraordinary pageant extending from the first Sunday of Advent to Twelfth Night and even longer. In recalling German Christmas, we encounter many practices which are common to other countries.

Holly leaves were referred to as "he" or "she," according to the presence or absence of prickles on a leaf. Smooth-edged kinds were called "she" holly, while those that were heavily spined were referred to as "he." Whichever kind was gathered in greater quantity for holiday decoration indicated who would rule the household for the coming year.

A charming bit of lore dating from the fifteenth century was associated with apple trees which burst into bloom at Christmas, sometimes even producing small fruits. In Nuremberg, pilgrimages used to be made to view a miraculous tree that "bore apples the size of a thumb" on the night of Christ's birth.

Greece

December, the time of storms and tempests, is the month of St. Nicholas, patron of seamen. His feast, which occurs on December 6th, is observed with great devotion. According to tradition, his clothes are always drenched with brine, his beard drips with sea water, and his brow is covered with perspiration because of his efforts to rescue sinking ships from the angry waves.

Because St. Nicholas is master of wind and tempest, no Greek ship travels without his icon on board. Before putting out to sea, seamen always take with them a dish of *kollyva* (boiled wheat grain). If the ship encounters rough seas, they cast *kollyva* on the water, saying, "Dear St. Nicholas, cease your rush." Faith in the saint's miracle powers has made his name popular throughout Greece, and many churches have been dedicated to him, especially on the islands and along the coast. Everywhere his icons are literally covered with silver *ex-votos* (tokens) representing ships. When a ship is in danger, in praying her skipper makes a solemn promise to bring St. Nicholas a silver or gold *ex-voto*, representing his ship, if he reaches land safely. Both the skipper and his sailors carry their offering to church barefooted, then a service is held and the *ex-voto* is hung on the icon of the saint. Thus, in Greece, St. Nicholas, the great protector, is a figure of much more significance than as a mere bringer of gifts and goodies to children as he is best known in the West.

Though Easter outranks Christmas as a feast day in Greece, the Christmas

53

season is observed as a religious festival and many ancient customs are linked with the birth of Christ. At the break of day on Christmas morning, children in the villages go from house to house singing the *kalanda* (carols), with the boys in the group providing a rhythmical accompaniment on their small metal triangles and tiny clay drums. The *kalanda* not only tell of the birth of the Christ Child but also include good wishes and praise for the master and mistress of the house and other members of the family.

Since the long four-week fast of Advent is over, elaborate preparations are made for the Christmas table. This is the time when the pig, having been fattened since midsummer, is slaughtered. Although pork is the staple dish of the Christmas meal, chicken is eaten in some villages and the pig is killed the day after Christmas. Every housewife bakes a *christopsomo* (Christ-bread), which is decorated with elaborate frosted ornaments, usually representing some aspect of the family occupation.

At Drymos in Macedonia, the farmer's Christmas loaf usually bears a plow and oxen, a wine barrel, and a house. The shepherd's wife uses lambs, kids, and a sheepfold to decorate her loaf. There are special buns for the cattle and the hens, baked in a variety of shapes.

In the Kozani area, a bun dedicated to the land and the sheep, made in the shape of a harness, is kept in the house all year, nailed to the wall. Buns dedicated to the cattle are usually reduced to crumbs, salted, and given to the beasts to eat as a protection against illness.

On the eve of the great day, when the table is ceremoniously laid, the housewife first places thereon the Christmas loaf and a pot of honey. Around it she arranges various dried fruits, walnuts, hazelnuts, almonds, and similar sweets. Then the master of the house makes the sign of the cross over the loaf with his knife, wishes everyone *chronia polla,* cuts the loaf, and gives each member of the family a slice. Honey is eaten first, after which the family lift the table three times with their hands. Then several other dishes are served, varying according to the region.

At Sinope in Pontus, on Christmas Eve it is the custom to insert a sprig of olive in the center of the Christmas loaf. On the sprig are hung dried figs, apples, and oranges. When the family takes its place at the table, they lift it three times saying: "Christ is born, joy has come to the world—Our Lady's table, Mary's table." When the meal is finished, the decorated Christmas loaf is placed on a shelf or hung in front of the household icons, olive branch and all, where it remains until Epiphany. Then it is taken down and eaten.

In the village of Simitli near Raidestos in Thrace, the housewife prepares nine different dishes on Christmas Eve. These are set on a low table and burning incense is swung over them, after which they are placed in front of the household icons so that Mary may eat and be content.

At Koroni in Messenia, the first slice from the Christmas loaf is given to the first beggar who happens to pass by. Since the bits and crumbs left from Christmas dinner are considered sacred, they are scattered near the roots of the fruit trees. "Even if the tree has been persistently barren, it will bear fruit next season without fail," is the belief.

54

In the rural areas of Greece, many practices intended to assure good crops are connected with the hearth. Thus, the plowshare and the Christmas table are placed near it. The Christmas cake is set in the center of the table and covered with a plate filled with wheat grain, garlic, silver coins, pomegranates, dried fruit, grapes, watermelon, and a glass of wine in which the housewife dips the *Kallikantzaros* buns. Family and guests drink wine, wishing each other "a good year." It is believed that these practices will protect the cattle from evil and ensure good crops and prosperity for the household. The plowshare is placed close to the fire, and the smoking embers are used instead of incense to bless the Christmas cake. Then the censer is carried to the stable and the sheepfold, where it is swung over the cattle and sheep and farming tools. This is done three times a year: at Christmas, on New Year's Day, and again at Epiphany.

In some villages, the women stay up all Christmas night to see the heavens bursting in glory, and they believe that any wish made at this time will come true. At Kios, near the Sea of Marmora, on Christmas Eve it was the custom of the village girls to gather at a friend's house, open the shutters, and place a sprig of dried basil in a basin of water on the windowsill, along with an icon of the Virgin Mary. They censed the basin and the whole room, read and sang Christmas hymns, glancing at intervals through the window in the direction of the East. It was believed that, if they were true Christians, at the moment of Christ's birth, they would see a great flash like lightning on the horizon. Some girls are said to have had visions of the Virgin Mary herself, holding Jesus in her arms.

This is also a good time for weather forecasting. In Thrace, the notion was held that an abundance of snow at Christmas signified good summer crops.

During the twelve-day period from Christmas to Epiphany, when it is believed that the "waters are unchristened, unhallowed," the *Kallikantzaroi* make their appearance on earth. They are best described as a species of goblin or a kind of spirit, who appear only at Christmas, emerging from the bowels of the earth. In *Greek Calendar Customs,* George A. Megas has written: "All year round, equipped with axes, they strive to cut away the (world) tree which supports the earth; but by the time they have nearly done, Christ is born, the tree grows anew, and the spirits leap to the surface of the earth in a rage.

"Popular imagination has given the *Kallikantzaroi* numerous and varied shapes. According to some people, 'they are like human beings, only dark and ugly, very tall, and wear iron clogs.' Others think of them as being 'very swarthy, with red eyes, cleft hooves, monkeys' arms, and bodies covered with hair.' Still others picture them as 'lame, squint-eyed creatures, very stupid . . .' They feed on worms, frogs, snakes, etc. They slip into people's houses through the chimney; they make water on the fire, ride astride people's backs, force them to dance, and pester them in every imaginable way."

Many curious notions are associated with children born at Christmas, since it is supposed that they turn into these strange creatures. Hence, if a child is born at Christmas, his mother must bind him in garlic tresses or straw to prevent him from joining the *Kallikantzaroi.* Another way of preventing this affiliation is to singe the child's toenails, for he cannot become a *Kallikantzaros* without toenails.

55

Nicholas Politis, noted scholar of Greek folklore, suggests that the *Kallikant-zaroi* are the creation of neo-Hellenic mythology. He points out that the twelve days from Christmas to Epiphany have always been a time of intensive masquerading, and that it was the custom of masqueraders to terrify people. Some people believe that these strange creatures are linked with the souls of the departed who return to earth once a year. For example, the people of Pharasa long believed that during the twelve days of Christmas the dead visited houses at night, entering through the chimney. Thus, incense was burned in the fire to ward them off. Another theory has it that they were souls residing in Hades, who returned to earth, according to ancient Greek belief, during the Anthesteria festival (when Hades opened its gates) and tormented the living. They befouled food, and for this reason the ancient Athenians used to surround their temples with red thread, making magic circles which the souls of the dead could not cross, they would smear their front doors with pitch, and chew boxthorn, in order to prevent the souls of the dead from entering their temples, their houses, or their bodies.

Even today, fear of *Kallikantzaroi* gives rise to similar protective measures. The lower jaw of a pig (which is supposed to have protective powers) is hung behind the front door or inside the chimney. Another practice is to throw a handful of salt or an old shoe into the fireplace, for the bursting noise and the stench caused by the burning salt or leather is believed to keep them away.

The chief means of keeping them away from the home is fire, which is thought to be unfavorable to evil spirits. Thus, the hearth is kept ablaze day and night throughout the twelve days of Christmas, with a stout log hewn from a thorny tree burning there. In Greece it is called the Christmas log, the twelve-day log, or *skarkantzalos*. Before it is placed on the hearth, it is sprinkled with various kinds of dried fruits. Further, the charred wood and ashes left in the grate are thought to have protective powers, and are used to preserve the house and the land from all evil—demons, bugs, and hail. Sometimes two or more logs are thrown into the fire. Placed on the grate in pairs and lighted together, this practice is called the "coupling of fire." Certain wild plants are known to make loud bursting noises and thick smoke when burning. For this reason wild asparagus, pine, thistle, and other plants are often thrown into the fire to drive away the demons. In northeastern Greece, bonfires are lighted in village squares on Christmas Eve for the same reason.

In many villages, from Christmas to Epiphany, during the time the waters are blessed, villagers never go out into the street without carrying a candle or a torch. They firmly believe that the only effective way of dispersing the *Kallikantzaroi* is by blessing the waters at Epiphany. Then all evil spirits scuttle away in a hurry, pursued by the priest's sprinkler (a cluster of sweet basil dipped in holy water). As they leave the world of the living, they whisper to each other: "Let us go, let us go—for here comes the blasted priest—with his sprinkler and holy water."

Holland

Holland is truly the land of St. Nicholas—so much so that even the chilly, drizzly, and dreary climate of early December is referred to as "real St. Nicholas weather." On St. Nicholas Eve, December 5th, there is hardly a family in Holland that does not, in one way or another, pay tribute to the "Old Bishop" and his servant Black Peter with a party or some kind of social gathering. Usually, presents abound and tables are laden with candies, cookies, cakes, and plenty of hot chocolate. St. Nicholas and Black Peter usually make their appearance, and everywhere their spirit is felt.

For days and even weeks beforehand, young and old are busily engaged in shopping, writing St. Nicholas rhymes, wrapping packages, and getting ready for the great day. As Henriette Van Nierop has expressed it in *Santa Claus, the Dutch Way:* "St. Nicholas Eve is a celebration of light-hearted spirit, rather than one of deeper meaning, like Christmas. To Hollanders, *Sinterklaas,* as it is called, is such an accepted event in their lives that most of them do not even question how it all came about, and how St. Nick assumed his present form as benefactor and friend of all children."

In medieval legend, St. Nicholas was actually a composite figure representing two bishops, both of whom came from Lycia in Asia Minor, and that image has not changed materially over the centuries. One, Nicholas of Myra, was an extraordinary churchman in the fourth century; the other, Nicholas of Pinora, died in 564. Both were important historical figures who lived so many hundreds of years ago that much of what is known about them is based on tradition and legend. Long, long ago these two men named Nicholas became merged into a kind of symbol—a saintly miracle worker to whom the Greek Orthodox Church turned for protection against dangers and catastrophes. However, it is the Bishop of Myra whose deeds and acts are best known.

A thousand years ago, when Myra fell into the hands of the Mohammedans, the treasured bones of St. Nicholas were taken to Bari in southern Italy and there interred. An impressive church was erected over his grave, and it became the center of St. Nicholas worship. Since Bari was a seaport, St. Nicholas became the patron of sailors, and thus the cult which developed around him was spread over western and northern Europe. As his popularity increased, in practically all of the harbor cities bordering the coastline of western and northern Europe, and the rivers as well, churches were built dedicated to St. Nicholas. Looking back six hundred years, we find that Holland, with its long coastline, its many wide rivers, and its seafaring population, counted no less than twenty-three edifices bearing his name. Many of these are still used as places of worship, although in Holland, since the Reformation, a number of them have been converted to use by Protestant congregations. Gradually, St. Nicholas became the patron of craftsmen other than those who sailed the seas. He extended his good deeds to those in the field of navigation, becoming the patron of a number of Dutch merchant guilds.

In the fourteenth century, choirboys in the various churches dedicated to St. Nicholas were given gifts of money and a special holiday on December 6th,

Sinter Klaas (as St. Nicholas is called in Holland) reads a favorable report of three happy youngsters who have earned a clean slate and can expect their reward in gifts aplenty. *Courtesy Particam, Amsterdam.*

During the weeks before the celebration on the eve of his birthday, December 5th, St. Nicholas and his faithful "Black Peter" walk the roofs and listen in the chimneys, to find out whether the children *and* the grown-ups are deserving of presents. *Courtesy Particam, Amsterdam.*

A tense moment as Sinter Klaas reviews the record. *Courtesy Netherlands Information Service.*

Blowing out the candles on the tree is part of the fun of Christmas. *Courtesy De Arbeiderspers.*

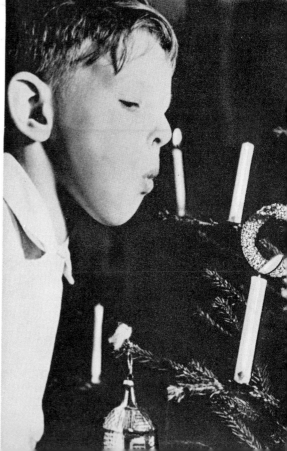

the birthday of the good bishop. It was their custom to choose a "bishop" from their own group who, dressed in costume complete with mitre and crosier, led a procession of boys through the streets begging for "bishop money." Half of the contributions received were spent for candles for the church; the other half for candy. Later, as with many popular religious events, these processions degenerated, the child-bishops and their choirboys turning into gangs who roamed the city streets and used the funds they collected for their own amusement. Thus, the practice was banned in the seventeenth century.

However, the spirit of St. Nicholas had become firmly entrenched in the convent schools. On his birthday, pupils of good intent were rewarded with gifts, while the lazy and the disobedient were punished with the birch rod, that indispensable instrument of discipline of the medieval world. One of the teachers dressed in appropriate costume—complete with long white beard, mitre, red mantle, and crosier—made the presence of the great benefactor very real to the children.

It was at this time that Black Peter appeared on the scene. During the Middle Ages, the Dutch commonly referred to the Devil as Black Man or Black Peter. A popular notion had it that, on his birthday, St. Nicholas chained the Devil and took him along as his servant. Peter's work consisted of dropping candy and gifts down the sooty chimneys into the children's shoes which were always placed by the fireside. They traveled from rooftop to rooftop all over Holland on their journey of good will. As time passed, Black Peter evolved into an amiable, grinning devil—a kind of jolly joker who assisted the "old man" by carrying the presents. Yet, he wielded a rod as well, and the sack which contained the goodies was used also to carry away naughty children. Even today, Black Peter has not lost his significance and represents the very antithesis of *Sinterklaas,* nor has the custom of placing shoes by the fireplace been forgotten.

This practice can be traced back five hundred years to records found in the ledgers of many of the St. Nicholas churches. Regular entries were made on December 6th designating the cost of several pairs of shoes containing money which were distributed to the poor in the name of the great saint. The custom of giving shoes with hidden treasures is said to have originated in the old legend in which St. Nicholas dropped dowries into the shoes of three pretty girls whose penurious father had sent them out to seek their own fortunes.

Accordingly, *Sinterklaas* became a popular symbol and is so recognized by all Hollanders—regardless of creed. As the birthday observance of St. Nicholas became steeped in custom and tradition, so too Dutch painters, composers, and writers have left us their interpretations on canvas, in print, and in countless folk songs which add to the luster and fame of the great man. Traditional candies and cookies have an important place in the observance, and the famous painting of the seventeenth-century Dutch master Jan Steen illustrates the special *taai-taai* and *speculaas* pastries which continue to be favorites during the *Sinterklaas* season.

When the Dutch settlers came to America in the seventeenth century, they brought with them devotion of long standing to their venerated old bishop, *Sinterklaas*. Later, through British influence, Father Christmas—the merry, rolypoly, Falstaffian figure in high boots—became known in the Colonies. Eventually, these two beloved figures, both commemorated in December, were merged into a single symbol of generosity. The rotund figure of Father Christmas remained, but he acquired a Dutch name—Santa Claus—derived from *Sinterklaas,* and was portrayed as a jolly Dutch burgher.

Toward the end of November of each year, St. Nicholas and his faithful servant Peter are anxiously awaited everywhere in Holland. Young and old, people of every denomination, from all walks of life, start acting mysteriously, shutting themselves in their rooms, slamming doors in other people's faces, and stuffing cotton in their ears while trying to compose rhymes. This is part of the every-day ritual prior to the arrival of St. Nicholas. Then, on the last Saturday in November, on everyone's lips we hear: "Look, there is the steamer bringing us St. Nick!" Seated on his great white horse and accompanied by his faithful servant Peter, St. Nicholas arrives by steamer in Amsterdam harbor (and in other harbor cities as well), cheered by literally thousands of children and adults. Traffic is a complete snarl, for the police are cheering too. Streetcars stop as conductors and passengers crane their necks for a glimpse of the celebrated visitor. In the midst of all this excitement the mayor, in official attire complete with silver chain of office, becomes the first Dutch citizen to greet the Bishop Nicholas. Resplendent in his elaborate bishop's robe with mitre and crosier, he descends the gangplank seated on his proud white steed, amid great pomp. Peter, in puffed velvet breeches and a plumed beret, typical of the fashion of sixteenth-century Spain, with a sack on his shoulder and a birch rod in his hand, hovers around to see that all is well with his beloved master.

Amid deafening cheers and with all the church bells ringing, the parade begins. First comes a motorcade of the police force and a brass band, followed by St. Nick on horseback wrapped in his scarlet mantle, with Peter walking by his side. The mayor and other city dignitaries follow in their cars, preceding countless beautifully decorated floats, a cavalcade of the local student body, and more brass bands.

Slowly and solemnly the parade wends its way through the crowded streets until it stops in front of the royal palace in Amsterdam, where Queen Juliana stands with her two younger daughters to welcome the bishop. The Princesses Margriet and Marijke are surrounded by hundreds of school children singing St. Nicholas songs. Typical of all Dutch children, Margriet, although impressed, feels quite at ease. She has a large carrot which she feeds to the horse. But Marijke is a little nervous, and when St. Nick asks her to sing a song for him she looks at all those expectant faces around her—and then, suddenly, she finds her answer. In a very clear little voice she says, "I'll do that this evening by the chimney, St. Nicholas, when I put out my shoe." (This custom of giving an annual account of conduct stems from earlier centuries and is a practice that is still a significant part of childhood in Holland.) Gently and quietly St. Nick points out a few little flaws in Margriet's and Marijke's behavior during the past year. Both promise solemnly that it won't happen again, and the grinning Peter passes out candy to all the children in the group. Queen Juliana then offers her apologies that her two older daughters, Beatrix and Irene, were unable to be there that afternoon. "But," says Queen Juliana, "I've brought an extensive

60

written report on each of them—and as you know, St. Nicholas, they've both been very good this year. So I feel sure you won't forget them on December 5th." Both then shake hands with great dignity.

Then St. Nicholas moves on, to be welcomed by more cheering crowds and with more familiar, old-time songs. The parade finally ends in front of a large hotel, where St. Nicholas and Peter make their headquarters. Then the old bishop removes his beard and mitre, puts his crosier in a corner, and asks for a cup of tea!

All over Holland, St. Nicholas Eve parties provide the best of entertainment for young and old, particularly when the guests gather around the dining room table to get their "surprises." Every single gift must be accompanied by a verse or a bit of doggerel. Whether it is short or long depends on the rhyming talent of the giver, but this personal touch cannot be overlooked. The verse usually deals with the good points or the weaknesses of the recipient and each poem is signed by *Sinterklaas* since the giver must remain anonymous. In preparing the packages, imagination is given free rein. Pretty gift wrappings are definitely the wrong thing; rather, the gifts must be carefully camouflaged and made to look like something else. Therefore, the Dutch call them "surprises" instead of presents. Small gifts are concealed in potatoes dressed as dolls, in a pudding made of gaily colored starch, or in a glove filled with wet sand. Larger items are hidden in the coal cellar, in a box of rubbish, or among other boxes filled with shredded newspaper. A dressmaker's form or a broomstick elaborately dressed (representing somebody's beau or girl friend), a cauliflower or a head of cabbage are typical of the way in which gifts may be concealed. The greater the ingenuity in disguising and camouflaging, the greater the fun. As the expression has it, all Holland "goes mysterious" at this time of the year.

A stranger in Holland in early December may be somewhat startled to find an otherwise dignified business executive deeply absorbed in hiding a little package in a gelatin pudding or in a big sausage. Not so the executive's staff— they realize that their "boss" is preparing his wife's *Sinterklaas* "surprise," which he cannot do at home for fear that she will be wondering what he is doing in the kitchen. In a similar way, a tourist seated in the visitors' gallery of the Second Chamber of the Dutch Parliament would surely be astonished to hear the Speaker open a debate in original verse with a number of the members answering in rhyme! But this is what happens every year on the fifth of December, St. Nicholas Eve.

In Holland, Christmas is celebrated much like Thanksgiving in North America. Every family has a tree, houses are decorated with evergreens and holly, and it is a time for feasting. Yet, it is not a time for parties and there are no presents, for they were given on St. Nicholas Eve. The effect created with the candle-lit tree and other tapers throughout the house gives Dutch Christmas a warm and intimate atmosphere and a very special unforgettable fragrance.

Christmas Eve and Christmas morning are both devoted to church services, while the afternoon is spent in the family circle. This is the time for telling stories and singing carols. Dinner, usually served at seven o'clock, is a feast in every sense of the word. The day after Christmas—another general holiday

61

called Second Christmas Day—is spent in a somewhat gayer fashion. In recent years, it has been the fashion for the family to eat at a restaurant, mainly to give the housewife a rest from household duties.

Practically all Dutch music societies, radio ensembles, professional vocalists, and school choirs as well as amateur groups take part in some musical performance in churches, concert halls, and other available auditoriums. All Holland bursts forth in song to greet the Christ Child.

Ireland

While Ireland is not known for its wealth of Christmas traditions, this small country has contributed several Christmas customs which are popular today. As the countryfolk will tell you, St. Patrick brought Christmas to Ireland late in the fifth century, and they speak of the event as though it occurred only recently. As in the past, it continues to be observed with deep religious overtones. The manger scene has its place in homes and churches, and the Christmas tree, while seen occasionally, is obviously a feature of recent introduction. The glossy-leaved holly wreath with its showy clusters of red berries, popular as a door decoration in North America, can be traced to the early settlers from the south of Ireland who came to the United States at the time of the potato famine.

So, too, can the lighted candle placed in the window on Christmas Eve. According to one belief, the candle has long served as a symbol of welcome to Mary and Joseph who sought shelter in vain on that first Christmas Eve. The ceremony of lighting the candle is one of those simple ancient rituals during which prayers are said for the departed and the privilege of striking the match is usually given to a daughter named Mary. For centuries it has been a practice in many Irish villages to set the kitchen table after the evening meal on Christmas Eve. On it is placed a loaf of bread filled with caraway seeds and raisins, a pitcher of milk, and a large lighted candle. The door is left unlatched. Thus, hospitality is extended to the Holy Family or to any traveler who might be on the road.

The story of the abiding faith to which this nation has clung so tenaciously for countless years is reflected in the symbolism of the lighted candle in the window, which in large measure spells out the simple beauty of the Christmas story. This flickering symbol also served as a signal in times past to any priest seeking shelter and protection that he was welcome to come to the house to say Mass. In a more poetic vein, it was said that the candles were "kindled to guide the Angels who on Christmas night direct the New Born from the heavens."

On December 26th, St. Stephen's Day, boys in the small villages in the south and west of Ireland observe an age-old ritual as they go from house to house with a stuffed wren or one made of straw (attached to a sprig of furze), singing a simple ditty and expecting a gift of pennies to buy candy or to provide a party.

62

The Wren, the Wren, the King of All Birds,
St. Stephen's Day was caught in the furze,
Although he is small, his family is great
Open up, lady, and give us a "trate."

As the door is opened to give the "trate," the boys burst forth with a smile, dance a few steps, repeat the verse, and then move on to the next house, where they perform in similar fashion. Occasionally they blacken their faces with charcoal as a disguise.

St. Stephen's name and feast are highly regarded in many parts of Europe, including Sweden, France, the British Isles (particularly Ireland and Wales), and other countries as well. This great missionary (often incorrectly referred to as the first Christian martyr) is the patron of horses. There is a legend that, at the time of the Nativity, he was a servant of King Herod's. Having seen the Star of Bethlehem, he made his way to the manger and then forsook Herod for the service of the Christ Child. In the greater part of England, his feast day is largely overshadowed by the observance of Boxing Day.

Among the old folkways formerly observed was the tolling of the bell in the village church from eleven o'clock until midnight on Christmas Eve. This practice was referred to as "the Devil's funeral," for it was thought that the Devil died when Christ was born.

Carols, poems, and songs galore have always been a part of Irish folk expression at Christmas, and many of them, passed down from one generation to another, are still sung or recited around the peat fire by the country people. A delightful old tradition largely forgotten now was the making of round cakes filled with caraway seeds, one for each member of the family. Woe to the one whose cake broke in the baking or handling, for it indicated bad luck for him. From this belief came a Gaelic name for Christmas Eve, "Night of Cakes."

Maura Laverty, noted Irish novelist and scholar, recounts that not even Oliver Cromwell with all his edicts could keep housewives in Ireland from making their favorite mince pies at Christmas. Here, as elsewhere in Europe, the pies were baked originally in cradle-shaped tins suggesting the form of the manger. Three puddings are made for the holiday season: one each for Christmas, New Year's, and Twelfth Night. In making the "cake-of-the-year," no expense is spared. It is usually baked in late October and "left to mellow until a fortnight before Christmas, when it gets its thick coat of almond paste. A week later it is glorified with royal frosting and decorations."

Italy

Weatherwise, Christmas in Italy varies greatly according to region. In the countryside around Lake Maggiore and elsewhere in the Alps and Apennines, it is winter. Leafless trees dot the frost-encrusted fields and snow-capped mountains frame the cold landscape. However, each late December day, as darkness approaches, the bleakness is overshadowed by starry Christmas skies. Rome, on

63

the other hand, is likely to enjoy a taste of spring, with the sun urging its warmth on the renewal of growth. The reflected light on the laurel bushes is a welcome sight. Farther south, it is truly a time of sunshine, warm enough on the Riviera for sailing and even bathing in sheltered places.

Since legend has it that it was to this land that the remnants of the manger at Bethlehem were brought in the early Christian centuries, it is perhaps not surprising that St. Francis should have renewed its spirit and meaning in the Umbrian Hills thirteen centuries later. Actually, Christmas had been celebrated as a great feast day for nearly a thousand years when Francis of Assisi appeared before a great throng at Greccio on Christmas Eve in 1223. Often described as "the most saintly of Italians and the most Italian of all the saints," Francis personified the very essence of humility as set forth by Nesta de Robeck in her delightful little book, *Saint Francis—The Herald of the Great King.*

"Shortly before Christmas he was back on Monte Rainerio and sent for a friend, Giovanni Vellita, and told him to prepare for the feast in the hermitage of Greccio, which was another of Francis's favorite mountain retreats. 'I desire to represent the birth of that Child in Bethlehem in such a way that with our bodily eyes we may see all that He suffered for lack of the necessities for a newborn babe, and how He lay in the manger between the ox and ass.'

"For Francis Christmas had always been the 'feast of feasts,' the feast of light and hope, of peace and joy and brotherly love, the day when 'Heaven and earth are made one,' when God 'condescended to be fed by human love.' He would have liked to see every poor man handsomely entertained, and every ox and ass be treated to double rations, and corn scattered for the birds. Christmas was the feast of Lady Poverty, and when at dinner a brother spoke of the poverty suffered by Christ and His Mother in Bethlehem, Francis, weeping for compassion, would no longer sit at the table, but finished his food crouching on the floor. He wanted, not to preach a sermon on poverty, but to illustrate once again for himself and for every brother what was the poverty of Christ.

"Giovanni willingly fell in with Francis's plan and arranged a manger filled with hay, and sent an invitation to all the friars and people of the neighborhood; 'and many brothers and good people came to Greccio during that night when the weather also was most beautiful. A great quantity of lights had been kindled, many songs and hymns were sung with great solemnity by the many brothers, so that all the wood echoed with the sound, and the man of God stood before the manger filled with the utmost joy, and shedding tears of devotion and compassion.'

"By his order the manger had been so arranged that Mass was celebrated on it, and blessed Francis the Levite of Christ sang the Gospel, and preached to the people on the Nativity of Christ our King, and when he pronounced His Name with infinite tenderness and love, he called Him 'The Little Babe of Bethlehem.' Saint Bonaventure goes on to tell of the vision of Giovanni who saw a seemingly lifeless child in the manger until Francis approached and woke him, 'nor was this vision untrue, for by the grace of God through His servant Blessed Francis, Christ was awakened in many hearts where formerly He slept. . . . Greccio was transformed almost into a second Bethlehem and that wonderful night seemed like the fullest day to both man and beast for the joy they felt at the renewing of the mystery.'

64

"Francis had succeeded in his wish that this particular Christmas celebration should 'move the people to greater devotion'; he had given new life to the crib of the Nativity plays, and his inspiration is still alive in every Christmas Crib in every church and home."

St. Francis not only brought a new kind of glory to the Christmas crib, he also paved the way for artisans and craftsmen to make miniature manger scenes for their own homes, and the crib-art spirit spread over all of Europe. Entire families participated in making these figures from wood or clay and arranging them to create little replicas of the Holy Land according to their own imaginations. Soon they were fashioning entire villages in miniature which often were more like their own communities than far-off Bethlehem.

In Naples, beginning in the eighteenth century, the Christmas crib, or *presepio* as it is called in Italy, developed into a popular art. Workers in the trade were known as *figurari,* and the crib figures which they made were called *pastori.* The story of the fad that developed reads like a fairy tale. Two men of widely different backgrounds, the Bourbon king Carlo III and a Dominican friar, Gregorio Maria Rocco, paved the way for a fascinating pastime that proved also to be a prosperous business enterprise. Carlo III had a passion for things mechanical and took great pleasure in making elaborate settings for the Nativity scene which was set up in his castle each year on Christmas Eve. Normally, such matters were attended to by the servants of the household, but such was not the case with King Carlo. The queen shared her husband's enthusiasm, and, together with her ladies-in-waiting, made the costumes for the various figures. It is reported that one of the Magi in King Carlo's *presepio* wore a miniature reproduction of his mantle as Grand Master of the Order of St. Gennaro.

Members of the court took up the hobby of their king and soon the making of *presepi* (plural of *presepio*) assumed social as well as religious significance. The nobility vied with one another in making these cribs, and it became fashionable to visit the homes of those who had built exceptional *presepi.* This hobby became the talk of the realm. In Naples the *presepio* became truly a dream right out of paradise, imbued with all the florid color of Neapolitan elegance. Sometimes the entire cycle or several scenes of the Nativity story were depicted. Especially popular were the episodes featuring the shepherds, the Magi, and the incident at the inn.

In *The Christmas Crib,* Nesta de Robeck wrote: "The scene of the inn gave the Figurari a chance they certainly made the most of; there could be seen every variety of macaroni and fish, sausages and wines from Ischia or Capri, while a countryman unloads a cart of victuals, a salesman displays his goods, beggars hold out a hand, minstrels play the guitar or hurdy-gurdy, and the guests eat and drink and gamble. It is an 'allegro con brio' from a Neapolitan opera and it is continued in the procession of the Kings decked out like princes from the Arabian Nights, laden with jeweled gifts, accompanied by slaves, camels, elephants, monkeys, horses, birds, and dogs, and this colorful cavalcade was completed by another of beautiful eastern princesses known as Georgine. The great ladies and gentlemen of Naples were to be found in the Crib alongside every kind of person from every province, cityfolk and countryfolk, all dressed in the right clothes, and in a setting which included every conceivable object known to daily life, each and all represented in perfect miniature models. No wonder

65

Christmas Crib arranged by Mary Alice Roche using figures carved in the Italian Tyrol.
Courtesy John Roche.

that the presepio gave work to such a host of people, of all the professions and arts."

The common folk too became interested, largely through the influence of the Dominican friar, Gregorio Maria Rocco. This crusader for moral and civic betterment succeeded in establishing the city's first municipal lighting system. At the time, vice and crime were rampant in Naples. With inspired words and warm-hearted deeds, Brother Gregorio exhorted the citizens to build more than four hundred shrines in the darkest corners of the city streets. These shrines were lighted with votive lamps, the oil being supplied by the populace, who filled them as they went to pray. Rocco then made his way into the slums of the city, and when sermons and plain talk failed to reach the ears of the evildoers, he was known to chastise them with the persuasion of his staff and his large wooden rosary. Like St. Francis at an earlier date, Rocco held the Nativity story in great reverence and thought that its visual representation in the form of a *presepio* could not fail to have a chastening effect on the most hardened of sinners. Following the tradition set by King Carlo and the noble families of the kingdom, he launched a campaign urging every family in Naples, no matter how poor, to build a *presepio,* and he often helped his parishioners to make them.

With such impetus, it is easy to understand why the Christmas crib became so popular in Italy. Only in recent years has the Christmas tree begun to vie with it for prime position in the home during the festive season.

Another Franciscan, Jacopone da Todi, who was born shortly after the death of St. Francis, became known as the "minstrel of the Lord" for his poetry written in the popular tongue that humanized Christianity. His verses on the Nativity, described as the first outburst of Christmas joy written in the vernacular, were the beginning of the "carol spirit" as we know it today. With simple words, directness of thought, and warm feeling, Jacopone told the world that the Christ Child was "our sweet little brother" and that Mary "rocked and hushed her boy." From this heart-warming demonstration of sentiment, there emerged an entirely new concept of Christmas that was to be heard, felt, and loved everywhere in Christendom.

Little wonder, then, that Christmas is described as "the warmest and most intimate of all Italian holy days." It has often been stated that the Italian family is the strongest of all social units and that the child at birth is wrapped in a blanket of love and affection. Some readers might take issue with this, for are not children everywhere loved wholeheartedly for themselves, for the joy they bring, for their helplessness, and most of all for their beauty? But somehow this conviction on the part of many a proud Italian is borne out in innumerable ways. As the editors of *Gourmet* expressed it in an article entitled "An Italian Christmas": "On *Natale* the Babe of Bethlehem becomes a real child to be fondled and kissed. Perhaps Italians feel more deeply than others the wonder of the God who is at the same time a child needing to be fed and warmed and cherished.

"The birth of the Son of Man is the epitome of all human births as well, so *Natale* is celebrated with feasting and music and the joys that are of this earth. There is a very old bit of verse:

> Natale festeggialo coi tuoi
> Capo d'anno con chi vuoi,

67

which truly expresses the Italian tradition. You celebrate the New Year with whom you please, but Christmas only with your own. The day of the *Bambino,* the day that God was born as a little child, is spent throughout Italy in the simple human joyousness, the intimate affection of the family."

The great love that Italians have for their *presepi* is even displayed by the grocers in their windows. Against a mountain of hams and great columns of colored tins of food, they often place a manger scene carved out of butter. In fact, every conceivable way of expressing the artistic aspects of the Christmas season becomes the province of the food merchants at this season of the year. They literally vie with one another for the attention of their customers. The butcher, the fruit seller, and the baker embellish their wares to give them the greatest possible eye appeal. In Sicily, the Christmas cakes are so handsomely decorated with fruits and vegetables made of colored almond paste that the bakers' windows look more like greenhouses than bakeshops. Fresh fruit of various kinds lends itself to endless decorative possibilities and the fruiterer has more than the usual opportunity to display his skill with all the richness of color, form, and texture that nature has provided.

No particular dish is common to all of Italy at Christmas. Fruit, nuts, and wines of every kind are accepted parts of the Italian diet, but on this great feast when families gather annually for their best-loved holiday, time aplenty is spent around overflowing tables. Special breads such as *pan dolce, panettone, pan forte,* and others are in great demand at Christmas. In the south of Italy, in addition to the meat course, *capitone,* a kind of eel especially prepared for the occasion, frequently is served. Among the various sweets, *torrone* or nougat has long been a favorite. On Christmas Eve, families in Rome enjoy a late supper before midnight Mass, while in Bologna and the lower Po Valley Italians spend the evening enjoying *tortellini,* "smooth mounds of pastry filled with savory meat." On the other hand, abstemiousness is observed in the towns and villages in the Alps, where carols and conversation are interspersed with simple fare until after midnight.

In Rome, ten days before the end of Advent, Christmas formerly was heralded by the arrival of the Calabrian minstrels or *pifferari.* Their sylvan pipes (*zampogne*), which resemble the Scottish bagpipes, gave forth plaintive tones as they moved from street to street playing before the shrines of the Madonna. Invariably, they stopped at carpenter shops "to be polite to St. Joseph." Unfortunately, they are seldom seen now.

For a single lira, minstrels in Naples would pipe melodies of an entire novena (a different series of prayers for each of the nine days) before any householder's street Madonna. In Sicily, shepherds came down from the mountains and performed in a similar fashion accompanied by the cello and the violin. In some regions, a small orchestra provided the music for the nine-day devotion in which everyone in the village took part. Henry Wadsworth Longfellow was greatly impressed with many of these simple prayers and translated some of them. Among the verses is this one:

> When Christ was born in Bethlehem
> It was night, but seemed the noon of day.
> The stars whose light was pure and bright
> Shone with unwavering ray.
> But one, one glorious star
> Guided the Eastern Magi from afar.

The best-known Christmas legend in Italy is the story of Befana. Actually, there are several accounts that explain her presence and why she brings gifts or switches to Italian children at Epiphany. (Her name is believed to be a corruption of the word Epiphania.) To be sure, she is known in many countries by different names—in Russia she is called Babouschka. Was Befana a witch or merely a preoccupied old lady who was too greatly encumbered by her own household duties to assist the Wise Men when they sought her aid in locating the way to Bethlehem? In any case, the story is told that, after refusing assistance, she repented and set out in pursuit of the Wise Men. Failing to find them, she continues to wander about at Epiphany rewarding good children and threatening those who deserve punishment for their misdeeds. Befana is the great gift-bringer in Italy, but, unlike St. Nicholas, she comes quietly in inconspicuous garb. Yet, she is constantly on the lookout for young people who are given to bad conduct, and mothers continually warn their children that Befana will come to take them away if they persist in misbehaving. For those who are deserving, the reward is candy and gifts in their stockings on Epiphany—but for others it is a switch and a piece of coal.

A shepherd of Abruzzi.

Norway

In a land where midday shadows begin to lengthen in September, the "turning of the sun" at Yule-tide gave rise to celebrations in Scandinavia long before the eleventh century when Christianity reached Norway. Heathen beliefs linked with the return of the dead on this darkest of days, as well as the anxiety concerning the year to come, added an eerie touch to the rejoicing over the return of the light. Fertility rites and the worship of the goddess Freia were also a part of these festivities. When the cross of Christendom replaced Thor's hammer, many of the old practices were so blended with new customs that, as elsewhere in Scandinavia, Yule-tide festivities in Norway today represent a blend of Christian ritual, colored with scores of quaint and unique practices springing from pagan roots. For example, the marzipan pig, a game known as the "Christmas buck," and the preparation of the "elf's porridge" are part of the otherwise Christian festival.

Yule in Norway is not only a time for feasting with all the attendant preparation of the season, but also (as in all Scandinavia), an occasion for singing, dancing, parties, and visiting. On the farms, the year's slaughtering is delayed until immediately before Yule. The "Christmas pig," whose fattening has been carefully followed by all the family throughout the year, provides the basic holiday dishes: sausages in variety, hams, cutlets, fat and trimmings for *sylte*—even the feet, which are pickled in salt brine, make good eating.

Until a few generations ago, there were farms in Norway where old trees were served food on Christmas Eve, even as the animals were given special rations. In one instance, a mug of ale, a piece of meat, and a bowl of porridge were placed every Christmas Eve before a venerable oak standing in the farm-yard. While no specific belief was attached to this practice in later years, it was continued as a part of cherished Yule ceremonies on that particular farm.

More common today in various parts of Scandinavia is the bowl of porridge placed in the hayloft of the barn. This is the Christmas treat for the family's "barn elf," who claims the loft and stable as his own particular domain. Should he be overlooked, he would never cease to recall this oversight during the coming year: a harness strap might break just as the heavy sled began to move, a cow might kick just when the bucket was nearly full, or any one of a number of things might happen just at the wrong time. The old belief has long been that it is still best to be on the safe side.

No one in Norway joins in the holidays without a good scrubbing from top to toe. This custom—like many others of the Christmas season—stems from the day when people were convinced that the new year began with Christmas Day.

During World War II, when Norway was occupied, free Norwegian forces made it a point to slip through German coastal patrols to cut a Norwegian tree as a gift for the exiled King Haakon each year. The practice of sending a tree to England has persisted since the war, and each Christmas a huge Norwegian tree stands in London's Trafalgar Square—a gift from the Norwegian people. In times past, tradition was generally centered around the Yule log, which was frequently an entire tree trunk dragged into the room with the butt resting in

This Christmas cookie from Czechoslovakia resembles a pretzel in its hardness. *Courtesy Elizabeth B. Freeman.*

This elaborately sculptured Norwegian Christmas cookie reflects the skill of country housewives. *Courtesy Norwegian Information Service.*

Gingerbread house with nineteenth-century figures of Santa Claus and Belsnickle. *Courtesy Abby Aldrich Rockefeller Folk Art Collection.*

the fireplace. It burned and smouldered during the whole of the Yule season, gradually being pushed farther onto the hearth as the end burned away.

While lighted candles have always been a part of the Norwegian Christmas, according to tradition they have always been placed in candleholders rather than on the tree. It was often a practice to have a candle for each member of the family, and in bygone days the light of each candle was thought to have particular powers over any person or object on which it shone. Formerly, on Christmas Eve in farm areas, the Christmas candle was carried through the yard, through the barn, and into the stable—and the farmer sang and made the sign of the cross in the hair of the cattle to ensure good fortune and good health during the coming year.

During recent years, the popularity of St. Nicholas and Santa Claus has led to the resurrection of an ancient Norse figure in the form of the gift-bringer *Julesvenn*. In ancient times, he was one of the mystical visitors on Christmas Eve who hid a tuft of "lucky" barley stalks in the house to be discovered on Christmas morning. Now he has been called back once more to bring gifts on Christmas Eve.

Little straw dolls, figures, and ornaments are always sold in Norwegian shops during the Christmas season. In days when the floors of Norwegian homes were made of packed earth, it was the custom to spread fresh straw thereon prior to Christmas. During the holy season's festivities it lay there, absorbing the mystical candlelight, the various rituals. In short, it became a part of the season's accoutrements—acquiring in time certain mystical qualities of its own. On Christmas Eve—when it was considered dangerous to sleep alone—the whole family (including servants and hired hands) slept on the floor in the Christmas straw, protected there against the evil thought to be abroad. This, too, was a sort of equality ritual where master and servant found themselves on equal levels on this one night of the year. After the Christmas season, the straw was gathered up and strewn on the fields as an omen of good harvest for the year to come. Although an insignificant part of the present-day Norwegian Christmas, the symbolism of the straw still remains.

Coffee and cakes, usually all fourteen different kinds, are part of the Christmas tree celebration. Delicacies may include *julekake* (a cake-like bread with citron); *hjortetakk,* doughnut-like cakes in an "e" shape; *berlinerkranser* in much the same shape, though not fried in fat; and a small fat-fried cookie called *fattigmann*. The name of the last cake, which means "poor man's cake" is slightly misleading, since quantities of eggs, butter, and fine flour go into its making. The name may imply that the maker can expect to be a "poor man" by the time he has made the cakes . . .

Poland

In Poland, as in many of the Slavic countries, the Star of Bethlehem is a dominant symbol around which the observance of Christmas revolves. The gleam of the first star in the evening sky on Christmas Eve means that the long fast of Advent is over. When the evening meal is served, small white wafers (*oplatki*) are eaten by each member of the family. This time-honored practice of the breaking of bread, symbolizing peace and friendship, takes its inspiration from the Sacred Host served at Holy Communion. Formerly, the clergy distributed packages of these wafers, made of white flour and water, to each family in the village. Available in quantity, they were often sent to friends and relatives in the same manner as Christmas greetings. Both the food served on Christmas Eve and the candles used at that time were blessed by the village priest, who called at the various homes to perform this simple ceremony; in some communities, it was taken in baskets to the church for the blessing. A vacant chair at the table indicated that a place had been set for the Christ Child, who the family devoutly believed was present in spirit.

After supper, the Star Man (sometimes the village priest in disguise or some well-informed neighbor) appeared to examine the children in their catechism. Those who responded with correct answers were given token presents, but those who failed were given a reprimand by the Star Man. Children believed that the gifts came from the stars but were carried to them by the Wise Men, impersonated by three young men of the village, known as Star Boys. They carried an illuminated star and sang carols as they brought in the little gifts. (It is on December 6th that St. Nicholas showers the children with presents.) Usually, the Star Boys were accompanied by groups of young people dressed in animal costumes or as characters of the Nativity. Some of the animals represented were those that were present at the manger in Bethlehem, while others, based on old folk beliefs, were introduced for sheer amusement. This bit of burlesque offered an opportunity to call on the neighbors, for whom the performers sang carols and were given a treat in return.

Although the custom was not limited to Poland, the showing of the *Joselki* or mangers during the week between Christmas and New Year's Day was a charming bit of religious drama that reached back to earlier times. They were small traveling theaters much like the type used for puppet shows featuring Punch and Judy. One writer, describing them as "gorgeous with tinsel and candles," related that the marketplace in Cracow was a brilliant spectacle with the sidewalks lined with glittering *Joselki*. Episodes from the life of Christ were featured in these little peep shows, which were adapted from the old miracle and mystery plays.

Sheaves of wheat used as decoration in the corners of the rooms during the Christmas season were later scattered in the orchard near the fruit trees, with the hope that the forthcoming fruit crop would be abundant. Needless to say, these sheaves were welcomed by the birds at a time when food was scarce. A layer of straw placed on the family table under the cloth helped to create the atmosphere of the stable where the Christ Child was born. More straw,

73

scattered on the floor, served the same purpose. A small table placed before the family shrine contained the Christmas candles and special pastries baked for the festive season. *Pasterka,* the Mass of the Shepherds, is heard by the family on Christmas Eve at midnight.

On St. Sylvester's Eve, December 31st, according to an old Polish belief everyone is his own master, free to pursue his own desires. Often this is the time when old superstitions foretelling the future are enjoyed. Many of these age-old notions, inherited in Slavic culture, are described in the following chapter on Russia.

Russia

For centuries, that most versatile and generous of saints, Nicholas of Myra, has been the patron of Russia. It is claimed that Vladimir the Great, grand prince of Russia, went to Constantinople early in the eleventh century to be baptized and brought back tales of the wonders of Nicholas. Thus, Nicholas was chosen as the protector of a country that covers one sixth of the surface of the world. Among the many talents attributed to him are protection of the weak against the strong, the oppressed against the oppressor, and the poor against the rich. Many churches in Russia were dedicated to him, and his name has been a favorite for boys in every station of life from that of the lowliest peasant to the Tzar.

From Russia, the fame of St. Nicholas spread to the Lapps and the Samoyeds, who likewise adopted him. As in Greece and the Slavic nations, where the Orthodox Church is the predominant religion, his feast has been served with great devotion and dignity for hundreds of years, but in recent times the Revolution in Russia has produced many changes in religious ritual, customs, and manners. Yet, despite changes in the form of government or in the philosophic point of view of a nation, the indelible imprint of tradition is difficult to stamp out entirely. Little remains today of the old folkways that only a few decades ago were an intimate part of everyday life in Russia. Yet, who can say that they have been forgotten entirely?

The carols known as *Kolyádki,* which have their roots in pagan culture, are still enjoyed. Father Christmas, now known as Grandfather Frost, and the Christmas tree (at present referred to more commonly as the New Year tree) are relics of an earlier tradition, despite their new names.

In old Russia, it was Babouschka who brought the gifts to the children. She is the counterpart of the Italian Befana, the old woman who misdirected the Wise Men when they sought her aid on their way to Bethlehem and then later set out in search of them. Failing to find them, she has traveled about ever since, rewarding good children with presents. In Russia, it was said that she crept into each house quietly, carrying a lighted candle so that she might observe the children asleep.

With the appearance of the evening star on Christmas Eve, the Advent fast was over and the *Colatzia* or supper was served on a table with a layer of straw beneath the cloth, symbolizing the Christ Child's bed in the manger. In *The Christmas Book,* Francis X. Weiser tells that eating thin white wafers, sometimes with honey or syrup (known as the "bread of angels" in Lithuania) was an ancient family ritual on Christmas Eve in Russia, a practice still observed in many Slavic countries. Various episodes of the Nativity were imprinted on the wafers which the head of the family served to his wife and children as a symbol of love and peace. Following the meal, various members of the family paraded about the neighborhood singing carols, dressed in costumes representing bears, goats, and the stable animals present at Bethlehem. Children were told that *Kolya* (Nicholas) always placed wheat cakes on the windowsill for them on Christmas Eve. These had to be eaten on Christmas Day.

In Russia, in the days of the Tzars, a carol with the opening line "Glory be to God in heaven, Glory!" which called down blessings on the Tzar and his people, was sung. Clement Miles describes the rest of the ceremony as follows: "At the Christmas festival a table is covered with a cloth, and on it is set a dish or bowl (*blyudo*) containing water. The young people drop rings or other trinkets into the dish, which is afterwards covered with a cloth, and then the *Podblyudnuiya* songs commence. At the end of each song, one of the trinkets is drawn at random, and its owner deduces an omen from the nature of the words which have just been sung."

In bygone days, a white-robed maiden known as *Kolyáda* was driven in a sled from house to house on Christmas Eve. (She appears to be a parallel to the Christkind, familiar in Germany.) The young people who attended her sang carols as they traveled about and were rewarded with gifts. *Kolyáda,* the name for Christmas, comes from *Kalendae,* the winter festival observed in pagan times.

In various parts of eastern Europe, the Christmas season was the time for the singing of carols (known in Russia as *Kolyádki* and in other Slav countries by similar names). Usually, these verses had no connection with the Nativity, but some were Christianized in spirit. More often, however, the sun, the moon, the stars, and ancient pagan myths were introduced, the thoughts expressed being those of hope for abundant crops.

In Little Russia, families used to eat honey and porridge on Christmas Eve. They called it *koutia,* and cherished the custom since it distinguished them from the Great and the White Russians. Each dish was believed to represent the Holy Crib; first porridge was placed in it (putting straw in the manger); then each member of the family helped himself to honey and fruit, which symbolized the Babe (fruit for the body, honey for the spirit). Another old belief was centered around sheaves of corn which were piled upon a table, in the midst of which a large pie was placed. The father of the family took his seat behind the sheaves and asked his children if they could see him. "We cannot see you," they would reply. Then, in poetic language, the father made a speech stating that he hoped the corn would grow so high in his fields that he would be invisible to his children when he walked there at harvest-time.

A favorite sport among girls in country districts during the Christmas season was a game called "the burial of the gold." They formed a circle, with one girl in the center, and passed a gold ring from hand to hand while the maiden within

75

the circle tried to detect the direction in which the ring was moving. All the while the group continued to sing, "Gold I bury, gold I bury." Some folklore scholars believe that the ring represented the sun which was buried in the clouds during much of the winter.

Another form of superstition which provided no end of amusement involved five piles of grain which were placed on the kitchen floor. Each pile was given a name—such as hope, ring, charcoal, money, thread. Then a drowsy hen was brought in and allowed to walk around the kitchen. Whichever pile she moved to first indicated a particular trend for the future. Hope meant a long journey or the realization of a wish. The ring signified marriage; charcoal foretold death within the family; money was a sure sign of wealth. Thread, on the other hand, indicated a life of hard work. Many an old wives' tale was spun while this diversion was carried out and the young girls who looked on learned their share of folklore.

The Blessing of the Waters on Epiphany Eve is an impressive tradition familiar in North America because of its annual observance in many of our Russian Orthodox communities. Formerly, country people looked upon this rite as the banishing of "forest demons, sprites, and fairies, which were once the gods which the peasants worshipped." It was believed that these sprites (like the *Kallikantzaroi* in Greece) were the creatures which bewitched and vexed them during the long dark winter nights. The ceremony, performed by cutting a hole in the ice, was carried on with chanting, a procession, and an elaborate ceremonial.

Scotland

During the seventeenth century, when the Puritans dominated the government of Great Britain, a ban was placed on the celebration of Christmas, and since that time religious festivals have never been especially popular in Scotland. This is not to say that Christmas goes unnoticed in Scotland and is without its customs and traditions. But, on the whole, the day is observed quietly. A waxing moon was always considered more favorable for Christmas than a waning one. The housewife was unfortunate, indeed, who left any work undone at this season. No one retired before midnight on Christmas Eve; nor was the fire allowed to go out on this night lest the elves come down the chimney and dance in the ashes. A bonfire, dancing, and music on the bagpipes were considered a fitting prelude to Christmas dinner. These and other old beliefs were once a part of Scottish Christmas.

It is on New Year's Eve, or Hogmanay as it is known, that the celebration of the year takes place. The term Hogmanay is of remote origin and its meaning is not entirely clear. However, the word also refers to the oat cakes served at this time, as well as to the most popular of all Scottish holidays and the merrymaking that attends it. It has long been the time for the liveliest kind of celebrating—a blend of sentiment, song, and spirits that sometimes extends beyond the

76

accepted levels of decorum. As the great bells strike the hour of midnight in the church towers everywhere in Scotland, the lid is off. Shouting, handshaking, the drinking of toasts, dancing, music, and the warmest flow of good wishes imaginable greet the New Year. This season of feasting and frolicking has long been known as the "daft days." In the nineteenth century, when Scots in great numbers emigrated to England, America, and Australia, they banded together to celebrate in the spirit of Auld Lang Syne on this most auspicious of evenings, but, in the past few decades, the practice has largely died out.

Children have always had their fun, too, on Hogmanay. Housewives had to rise early to be ready with the bannocks (oat cakes) for the neighborhood children who came singing:

> Rise up, guid wife, and shak' yer feathers.
> Dinna think that we are beggars;
> We're only bairnies come to play.
> Rise up, an' gie's our hogmanay
> Hogmanay, trol-lol, trol-lol-lay!

New Year's Day was Cake Day to the young folk in Scotland, and they had no need for breakfast, having already eaten more than their share of oat cakes and other good things received as they went from house to house. Sometimes, men and boys went around with a piper, dressed in women's clothes, with their faces blackened. They were hardly satisfied with plain oat cakes or scones (as they are also called) and the noise that attended this frolic came to an end only when, too weary to "go it" any longer, they sang a carol of thanks. Carol also means a cake—a good-sized piece at that. Shortbread flavored with nuts or caraway and black buns were also favorites at this season.

Looking back to earlier times, we find that this was an appropriate time to burn juniper in the house and the stable to protect both the people and the animals from harm. Farm animals were always given extra rations of food at this season.

Good fortune and the New Year are synonymous everywhere. In Scotland and in the north of England particularly, the custom of "first footing" is an ancient one, still enjoyed in a variety of ways with all the warmth and joy of the season. (The "first foot," the bringer of good luck, is the first visitor of the New Year.) Traditionally, as Christina Hole records in *Christmas and Its Customs:* "He brings a piece of coal, a piece of bread and a little money or salt—magical gifts by which he ensures that the family he visits will have warmth, food and wealth throughout the year." If he carries a sprig of evergreen, he is most surely a person steeped in old-time lore, for this is a symbol of continuing life. Formerly, the "first footer" entered the house without speaking and went to the hearth to stir the fire before greeting anyone. All was silent until this ritual was finished, since the welcome visitor was the bringer of the "true luck."

A tall, dark, handsome man has always been the preferred type of "first footer," especially in the north of England, and, in some regions, a person of fair complexion or with red hair was considered unlucky to "let in" the New Year. The "lucky bird," as he was sometimes called, often was considered more desirable if he were a bachelor. By no means must he be flat-footed; rather, he must have a foot that "water runs under."

77

The appearance of a woman as first visitor was considered an ill omen, indeed. To assure the right situation, there was usually a family friend who knew what his obligations were and he performed his duties well. Domestic servants made it a practice to invite their suitors to be their "first foots." Among old Scottish families, it was considered highly complimentary to have their servants do them the honor and grandparents were pleased when their grandchildren "first footed" them. Groups of mummers and young folk with a desire to entertain often participated as well. In more recent times, the custom has been broadened so that the "first footer" (if he is worth his salt) has a warm kiss and a hug for all the women and a hearty handshake for the men. Refreshments are plentiful and a pleasant party makes the occasion one of great merriment.

Spain

Christmas Eve in Spain, known as *Noche-buena* or the Good Night, ushers in the birth of the Christ Child in a surprisingly festive manner. Today the torches, candles, and lamps that once provided picturesque lighting in town and city streets have all been replaced by the brighter glow of electricity, especially in the shopping districts. Crowds of young folks throng the streets expressing their gaiety in singing and dancing, in the same manner as did their parents and grandparents. Tambourines, guitars, gourd rattles, and castanets lend warmth and vitality to the excited chatter heard everywhere.

The home shrines are lighted at dusk and the *nacimientos* or manger scenes that have been set up previously in the best room of the house gleam with light. Delicacies like almond soup, truffled turkey, and chestnuts, cooked in a variety of ways, are ready to be served to visiting relatives.

Christmas Day is a time set aside primarily for family reunions, because it is the special season for the Holy Family. Singing and dancing around the *nacimiento* has long been a favorite pastime of the children during the holidays. Since this day is also the occasion for the family feast in Spain, friends usually are not invited but relatives galore are always present.

Every country has its favorite Christmas sweet or delicacy. In Spain it is *turrón,* a kind of nougat or almond candy that everyone eats. It is sold from door to door and varies in quality according to the maker and the ingredients used, but no one is too poor to eat his share of *turrón* at Christmas. A thousand years before the time of Christ the Carthaginians who came to Spain from Asia Minor used to offer gifts to one of their goddesses in the form of cakes. Some historians believe that this ancient custom may be the forerunner of the enjoyment of *turrón.*

Midnight Mass in the great cathedrals, and in country churches as well, serves as a royal welcome to the Christ Child. The people have in many cases traveled long distances to reach their parish churches and in other instances the city dwellers have been parading city streets for hours. Joy resounds as the rich tones

of the organ, implemented by the tambourine and the guitar, are blended with the spirited voices of the choir and the congregation.

Christmas Day is devoted to feasting, the exchange of gifts and greetings, and the traditional rite of the Urn of Fate, a practice that has survived since the days of the Romans. In some countries where this practice still exists, gifts are placed in a great bowl and drawn with much laughter and merriment. However, in Spain, names written on cards are drawn two at a time, with the wish and the hope that those thus paired off will be friendly during the coming year. In many instances, this old folkway is a kind of match-making ceremony, and sometimes, by maneuvering the names in the bowl, interested parties achieve their wish of being suitably paired off.

Visitors to Seville during the Christmas season find great delight in the picturesque atmosphere and the colorful touches of true Old World charm in the shops, on the streets, and in the churches, great and small. One is likely to meet a costumed figure representing one of the Wise Men as he makes his way to the shopping area where the streets are strung with colored lights alternating with choirs of angels, fashioned out of cardboard. In the late afternoon these avenues of commerce are closed to vehicles so that people may shop with ease and comfort.

Each year, as of old, booths are set up on the steps of the cathedral at Barcelona where *nacimiento* figures are sold, as well as greens and Christmas trees. In earlier centuries, it was customary to set up stalls for the sale of religious objects in connection with practically all church feasts or *ferias,* as they are known. (Originally, the word *feria* referred to a religious feast among the Romans, and according to Francis X. Weiser, author of *The Christmas Book,* it is believed to refer also to the Hebrew Sabbath or Day of Rest.)

Bringing in the Yule log with all the attendant fanfare of beating it with switches to ensure good fortune still has its appeal in some villages. The boys who do the hauling stop at neighboring houses along the way, where they receive chocolates, nuts, and other good things to eat to supply the needed energy to tug the heavy log home.

The feast of the Immaculate Conception, which takes place on December 8th, is observed for an entire week and serves as a fitting prelude to Christmas. Since the Virgin Mary is the patron of Spain, this special day dedicated to her and the week or octave following are observed on a most elaborate scale. In the northern regions of the country, the balconies of the houses are decorated with flowers, carpets, and flags, and candles are burned all night in the windows on the eve of the feast. In Seville's great cathedral, the largest Gothic structure of its kind in the world, a most unusual ceremony known as *Los Seises* or the "Dance of the Six" takes place. Since the dance in its various forms is so much a part of the life and the spirit of the Spanish people, it is easy to understand why choreography is performed as an act of reverence.

Centuries ago, before Spain was a nation, the Israelites danced before the Ark of the Covenant; there are those today who trace *Los Seises* back to this ancient source. Evolving from a popular folkway, the ceremony was adopted by the Roman Catholic Church hundreds of years ago, and in bygone days was presented on special feast days in many parts of Spain. Although originally

79

referred to as "the Sixes," there are now ten boys, trained under ecclesiastical direction. The performance is usually held at five o'clock following Vespers at Easter, on Corpus Christi, and the December Feast of the Immaculate Conception. For generations the presentation of this traditional dance has attracted great numbers of foreign visitors who travel long distances to see it performed.

Arthur Stanley Riggs has described *Los Seises* vividly in *The Spanish Pageant:* "Golden candle-light from the silver high altar flooded the chapel with mellow radiance that brought out the shadows Rembrandt-like; the huge rose-windows at each end of the transept burned in glorious colors in the waning afternoon sunlight; the *reja* threw black shadows on the dull stone floor; there was a great black patch in the crossing, where the spectators sat or knelt. The ceremony began to the accompaniment of organ and orchestra, the boys singing with voices shrilly sweet, as if their little throats would burst."

It has often been said that the Spanish have a sense of timelessness as it relates to things eternal. Nowhere is it more apparent than in the pomp and ritual of their religious ceremonies. Even today, all ten performers are dressed in modish pale blue satin with lace trim after the manner of page boys, complete with brimmed hats and plumes, all in the best baroque style of a more elegant era. Thus, the emotion experienced by those who gather to witness this liturgical drama is as unforgettable as the words of the simple hymn of praise:

> Hay, Jesus mio,
> tu amor me inflame;
> Hay, hay, Jesus mio,
> tu amor me inflame;
> Pues ha salido para inflamarme!
> Ven, amor mio;
> ven, y no tardes;
> ven como sueles a consolarme!

"Then came the dance, to the repetition of the song. And what a dance! a quaint, reverent series of posturings, not unlike the geisha dances of Japan. In some respects it suggested the lancers, in others the minuet. But each movement —line, star, double chain, or wheel—had a cryptic meaning and a religious purpose, the SS of the double chain, for example, indicating *Santissimo Sacramento.* Suddenly a sharp staccato rattle startled us, for we had not noticed castanets in the young hands. They side-stepped, reversed, sang, moved forward and back, whirled violently to position with a final triumphant roll of their castanets, knelt, bowed jerkily—boy fashion—to the altar, and the dance was done.

"The solemnity of the cathedral atmosphere, the richness of the archaic costumes, the perfect gravity and earnestness of the young performers, all give it the quality of a fitting part of the sumptuous ritual of the church, as natural as it is at first striking."

The fragrant flowers of spring bloom in Seville at Christmas while in the Catalonian villages of the Pyrenees the snow-capped mountains give Christmas a different kind of atmosphere and flavor. The thought has often been expressed that many Old World customs and traditions reflect an abounding sense of joy and a warm feeling of delight in simple things—birds, animals, flowers, trees. Linked with them is a feeling of peace and contentment that springs from the

80

very soil which the farmers till. In Catalonia, each year at Christmas they sing the glorious "Carol of the Birds" which the noted cellist Pablo Casals has made popular with audiences in recent years. In its naïve charm, this carol literally transports us back centuries to the time when the simple narrative of Christ's birth was explained to ordinary people in terms they could understand. Did not birds of the air sing for joy on that glorious night in Bethlehem?

A star rose in the sky
and glory from on high
did fill the night with splendor.
Came birds with joyful voice
to carol and rejoice with
songs so sweet and tender.
Came birds with joyful voice
to carol and rejoice with
songs so sweet and tender.

The eagle then did rise,
went flying through the skies,
to tell the wondrous story,
sang, Jesus, born is he,
from sin we are set free,
he brings us joy and glory.

The sparrow with delight
said, This is Christmas night,
our happiness revealing.
The sky with praises rang,
as finch and robin sang—
oh, what a happy feeling!

The lark upon the wing
said, Now it seems like spring,
no more is winter pressing;
for now a flower is born
whose fragrance on this morn
to earth brings heaven's blessing.

Sang magpie, thrush, and jay,
It seems the month of May
in answer to our yearning.
The trees again are green
and blossoms now are seen,
it is the spring returning!

The cuckoo sang, Come, come,
And celebrate the dawn
this glorious aurora.
The raven from his throat
then trilled a festive note
to the unexcelled Señora.

The partridge then confessed,
I want to build my nest
beneath that very gable
where I may see the Child
and watch whene'er he smiles
with Mary in that stable.

81

This and other beloved songs of joy, or *goigs*, are sung on the feast days of the year, each feast having its own special group of *goigs*. In Catalan villages, the carolers are known as Rosers, members of a confraternity of Our Lady of the Rosary. They organize the social activities of the community and are governed by officers whose position gives them a place of dignity and authority among their neighbors. In some villages, the *mayorales* serve for a year, beginning on Christmas Day.

In describing the spirit of the carols, Freda Morrill Abrams has written: "Catalan Christmas songs are gay as the sound of guitars and the dancing steps of the *sardana*, fragrant as honey or eucalyptus pod, sparkling as the snow on Mt. Canigou or the waves on the Costa Brava, and wondrous as a child finding a shimmering jelly-fish on the shore, or playing with little jewel-like pebbles thrown up by the sea as he listens to its song echoed by the birds in his mother's patio garden.

"The festival of Christmas in both its moods of holiday and holy day has captured the heart and soul of the Catalan. His poetic imagination has been inspired by the meeting of the relative and the eternal in Christmas, where God becomes more human, even vulnerable, and man more divine."

With delightful simplicity, in tableau fashion, the Catalan carols portray the numerous incidents relating to the birth of Christ, beginning with the story of the Annunciation.

One of the most appealing of them all is entitled "What Shall We Give to the Babe in the Manger?" How natural that they should answer by offering the good things that they themselves have harvested along their sunny Mediterranean coast: clusters of raisins, a basket of figs, olives and nuts, cream cheese and honey; and lastly a special Catalan gift, a song of love and joy. Along with a song, they join hands in a circle to offer a folk dance for the Child, while a young shepherd sings (*El Petit Vailet*):

> I am a shepherd boy,
> All tired on my way,
> With my shepherd's crook I come
> To see Jesus born today.
>
> *Chorus*
> Hosanna, hosanna, hosanna,
> Hosanna, we sing in our joy,
> Hosanna, for Joseph and Mary
> Have a darling little Boy.
>
> Here's some clothing I would give
> To the Baby lying there,
> It will help to keep you warm,
> Little Child with face so fair.
>
> If I had more things you need
> I would give you all I could,
> You may even have my crook,
> It is made of cherry wood.

The Magi hold a particular fascination for the children of Spain which is shared enthusiastically by their elders since this age-old folk tradition has a cherished link with the Bethlehem story. As the tale goes, each year the Wise

Men travel through Spain on their way to Bethlehem. To receive them properly, the children fill their shoes with straw before they retire on Epiphany Eve and for their efforts they find presents in them on the following morning.

Not only in Spain, but in Portugal and in Provence as well, it used to be customary to go out to meet the Magi on Epiphany Eve. Off to the edge of town or to the city gates young and old would trudge carrying cakes for the Kings, as well as straw, carrots, and a variety of foods for their servants and animals. Parents carried rattles, pans, bells, and horns to give the great caravan a warm-hearted welcome. Sometimes one of the men in the group carried a ladder which he climbed frequently in an effort to locate the Magi.

But, alas, these eager greeters never met the Magi, for they always seemed to approach the town by another road. Thus, the children ate the goodies, threw away the straw, and returned home weary and disappointed. Whereupon parents explained that the Kings were assembled at the great *nacimiento* in the village church. There the children went and found Gaspar, Melchior, and their beloved Balthazar presenting their gifts of gold, frankincense, and myrrh. (Spanish children have a great fondness for Balthazar and he is often depicted riding a donkey.) At the *nacimiento* it was the usual thing for the entire community who had gathered there to sing, "This morn I met the train of the Kings on the wide high road."

On Holy Innocents' Day, December 31st, boys light bonfires at the town gateways and select a mayor who enforces law and order by requiring citizens to clean the streets. Fines are imposed for various alleged offenses in order to collect money for the expenses of the celebration.

Wassailing the fruit trees is an annual holiday ceremony that still lingers in the Pyrenees. Children go from farm to farm where a child has been born during the previous year, singing and beating time with their heavy shoes. In return, gifts of food are expected and usually provided in abundance. Woe to the penurious housewife who neglects the appeal!

Sweden

Although the old expression, "Christmas lasts a month in Sweden," must not be taken literally, the festive season does begin on December 13th with the feast of St. Lucia and ends on January 13th, *Tjugondag Knut,* the day dedicated to St. Hilary. From Christmas Eve and until the New Year has been greeted, the wheels of commerce and everyday living, both real and metaphorical, slow down perceptibly, and there is much more thought of cosy pleasures in the mind of everybody than of real attention to business. In modern Sweden, ancient custom and folklore make this season a true festival of the home, with hospitality overflowing in every direction.

Especially in the rural sections, preparations for the Yule season, as it is called in the Scandinavian countries, are begun early in December, for no festival of the year is more greatly loved. The term "Yule" may have come from *hjul,* meaning wheel, which suggests the turning of the seasons. The introduction of Christianity to Sweden gave new significance to the observance of the winter solstice, but the old folkways, beliefs, and practices, as well as singing and dancing, have not been forgotten. For example, the Yule goat made of straw, known as a *Julbrock,* is a replica of Thor's goat on which the bringer of Christmas gifts rides. As Gunnar Edman has expressed it in *Swedish Christmas:* "Christmas is not only an idyll and the innocent joy of children. It is also that time when the blackness of mid-winter stands darkest over the earth; it is the time of the goblin, of the spirit, and the ghost."

Baking now becomes a kind of culinary ceremonial and a wide variety of buns, cakes, and loaves of many different kinds, shapes, and colors are made. These include wort bread, sweet and dark, the fragrant saffron loaves, as well as gingersnaps in the form of goblins, piglets, stars, and other patterns. Christmas cookies of elaborate design include the sowing cake, the cross bun, the twelve-hole kringle which looks like an elaborate pretzel, the minister's hair, and the church door, to name only a few. In ancient times, it was the practice to save one of these cookies until spring and then toss it in front of the plow to ensure a good harvest.

There are still old-time cooks who make headcheese and Christmas sausages at home, and there are those who still dip their own tallow candles for old times' sake. These practices, handed down like heirlooms from generation to generation, keep strong those links with the past which are not easily forgotten by those whose associations are close to the soil. To be sure, all these items can now be purchased in shops and department stores, as is the new custom in many parts of the world, but *home-made* is a magic word everywhere.

Just as Belgium, Holland, and other countries launch the season with St. Nicholas Day on December 6th, Sweden pays tribute to St. Lucia on December 13th. Early in the morning before daylight on this day, families all over Sweden are awakened by a "Lucia," usually the eldest daughter of the family, singing the ancient Sicilian song "Santa Lucia." Dressed in a white robe and wearing a crown of lighted candles surrounded by greenery, she presents a tray loaded with

84

coffee, saffron buns, and Christmas cookies to each member of the family, serving them while they are still in bed. The younger children of the family usually participate as followers of Lucia, wearing the traditional glittering star on the tips of their conelike hats.

Lucia, known as the "Queen of Light," was actually born in Sicily. As a young girl, on the eve of her marriage, she gave away her entire dowry to the poor of her village and publicly admitted that she had become a Christian. Accused of witchcraft, she died a martyr's death on December 13th, A.D. 304, under the edict of Emperor Diocletian. Later, she was canonized and thus received the name by which she is now known, St. Lucia. For her connection with Sweden we must turn to medieval legend and folklore. One account has it that Lucia brought food to the hungry people in one of Sweden's provinces during a time of famine. She was dressed in white and a luminous halo in the form of a crown of light encircled her head. It is this dramatic and appealing image that has been preserved over the centuries.

The appearance of the "Queen of Light" at this season, near the time of the winter solstice, seems most appropriate as symbolizing the return of light after the dark days. Actually, the winter solstice occurs on December 22nd rather than December 13th. The difference in dates is explained by the adoption of the Gregorian calendar in 1753, while Lucia's feast day is still celebrated on December 13th, according to the old Julian calendar. Thus, the belief is surrounded by deeper meaning since the return of light is a symbol of hope and charity to the Swedish people in keeping with the original tradition.

Primarily an occasion for family celebration, there is hardly a Swedish home where the day is not revered. In recent years, Lucia Day has evolved into a community festival observed in offices, factories, and schools. Every large Swedish community elects its own Lucia. The election, usually sponsored by a local newspaper, culminates in an elaborate parade, combined with fund raising for charity. In Stockholm, where hundreds of girls vie for the honor of becoming Lucia, the final election is made by popular vote, with ten candidates contending. On the evening of December 13th, the Stockholm Lucia and her attendants and followers parade the streets of the Swedish capital in gaily decorated carriages. The colorful parade is watched by thousands of spectators and winds up at Stockholm's famous City Hall, where a banquet is held, the highlight of which is the presentation of the Lucia Ornament. Since the annual Nobel Prize awarding ceremony takes place in Stockholm on December 10th, a Nobel Prize winner is usually on hand to make the presentation. It is not difficult to see a symbolical meaning in this: the ideals which prompted Alfred Nobel to make his famous donation for the betterment of mankind are also expressed in the present-day Lucia ceremony. In several cities in North America where there are large numbers of Swedish settlers, this tradition is widely known.

In Stockholm and in other Swedish cities, department stores hum with the same kind of bustle found in Paris, New York, and London. The main thoroughfares are hung with garlands of electric lights and the show windows are brightly illuminated, contrasting vividly with the lowering, dark sky, for at this time of the year there are not many hours of daylight in this North country. But Christ-

85

Lucia, the "Queen of Lights," is honored each year in Sweden on December 13th. This feast day opens the Christmas season with a parade and a gala celebration. *Courtesy Swedish National Travel Office.*

mas shopping is not exclusively limited to the big, modern shops. Dear to the hearts of young and old is the Christmas mart in the Stortorget Square, known as the medieval section of Stockholm. There gay, old-fashioned Christmas booths are set up, filled with every conceivable kind of hand-made article fashioned from wood, metal, or textile, as well as home-made candy in gay wrappers. In the center of the historic square, flanked by ancient gabled houses, rises a tall Christmas tree. On its branches hang large lanterns with real candles.

The crafts of Christmas are also featured at the fair held at Skansen, Stockholm's famous outdoor museum, folk park, and zoological garden. Ornaments for the tree, little straw goats, picturesque candelabra known as applesticks, quaint and brightly colored Dalecarlian wooden horses, rustic doilies, hand-woven baskets, and other attractive trinkets are typical of the items sold.

The Christmas tree has a place of prime importance in Sweden. Although generally considered a German custom, the Scandinavian world had its Yule tree in bygone centuries. It was brought indoors or placed near the entrance to the house, fresh, live, and green, as a symbol of man's eternal hope for another spring after the long cold winter. The evergreen tree has long been a symbol of immortality and hope. As one Swedish writer has expressed it: "Whole little forests of fresh spruces seem to grow overnight on the square and market places, and the business is brisk. This is a matter that concerns the whole family; and every member is consulted as to the size and shape of the tree. When the right one has been picked, be it a very modest or a large, wide-branched one, it is carried home by father or mother, with the children giving a helping hand." Then it is given its traditional place of honor in whichever of the living rooms will best accommodate it. Strangely enough, although Sweden is one of the most extensively electrified countries in the world, thousands of families still cling to the old-fashioned manner of lighting the tree with real candles. Tinsel, shiny red apples, a variety of ornaments, and a shining star or a miniature Swedish flag for accent at the top complete the picture. Red blobs of fragrant sealing wax are used to secure the gift wrappings around the presents. Swedish custom calls for a verse, usually in a humorous vein and of a nature that half reveals, half conceals the contents, to be affixed to each parcel.

Sons and daughters of Sweden, wherever they are at Christmas, recall that the high point of the holidays comes on Christmas Eve, *Julafton*. Daily occupations cease early as everyone hurries home to the midday meal. Old and young gather in the kitchen, which is bright with colored candlesticks and vases of flowers and fresh pine branches, for the dipping of bread in the pot known as *doppa i grytan*. On the stove simmers a large iron pot with the drippings of pork, sausage, and corned beef. Slices of wort bread are speared on forks and dipped into the liquid until they are thoroughly saturated, in remembrance of an ancient famine when the only food was dark bread and broth. When the dipping is over, luncheon is served.

Dusk comes early at this time of year and the wish for a white Christmas is usually fulfilled to give the season its natural setting and atmosphere. Dinner is an intimate family gathering, and a traditional menu is served in almost every home in Sweden. First comes a smorgasbord with ice-cold schnapps, or Akvavit, followed by *lutfisk* (sun-cured cod, served with a cream sauce), a rosy Christmas

ham, and a variety of breads and other good things. The meal is topped off with steaming rice pudding or porridge. In its midst an almond is hidden, and the belief is that the one who finds it will marry before the next year is up, but no provision is made for those who are already married!

Coffee, followed by almonds, candy, and raisins, is served in the living room, in close proximity to the Christmas tree. When the flickering white candles on the green branches are lighted, all electric illumination in the room is turned off. A rare and wonderful peace descends as every eye in quiet contemplation watches the glimmering flames. Then the gifts are distributed by *Jultomten,* as Kris Kringle or Santa Claus is known in Sweden.

According to Scandinavian tradition, *Jultomten* is a little gnome, the guardian of the household or farm. If the cows are to give milk freely during the next year and the buildings kept safe from floods and storms, it is imperative to remember *Jultomten* on Christmas Eve. Since he likes porridge, it was the custom in former times to place a big bowl in the hayloft for him to enjoy after he had made his last round of the barns and stables. Even today, this ceremony is observed. On farms, the cattle receive an extra portion of fodder, and for the birds in both town and country large sheaves of grain are put out on a pole in the snow—a Christmas tree for the birds. When it comes time to say good night, the parting wish is:

> May God bless your Christmas;
> May it last 'til Easter.

For centuries in Sweden, Christmas Day has been dedicated to religious observance and rest. The predawn service is perhaps most impressive and colorful in the country, where the people find great pleasure in driving to church in sleighs, weather permitting. While the night is still dark, churchgoers in some parts of the country light their way through the snowy, silent forests with flaring torches. This practice, followed in many of the colder parts of Europe, makes an unforgettable sight. Here and there the darkness is pricked by glowing dots, because on Christmas morn almost every house in Sweden has a lighted candle in each window. Between the tall pines and the spruce trees lies the country church, the candlelight shining invitingly through the stained glass windows. Close by, the worshippers toss their torches into a large pile which flickers in the dark night and casts its reflection on the snow. At the door the people are met by the organ notes of that inspiring Lutheran hymn, "All Hail the Beauteous Morning Star," while before them the altar shines with the radiance of hundreds of burning tapers.

St. Stephen's Day, December 26th, is known as the second day of Christmas. This day, which commemorates the patron of animals, is observed in a variety of ways in various parts of Europe. In Sweden, Stephen's men ride through various communities in the early morning to awaken the inhabitants. According to tradition, Stephen was among the first Christian missionaries who came to Sweden—about A.D. 1050. It is said that he had five horses—two red, two white, and one dappled. In his travels, he used them one at a time to carry him in the performance of his duties of spreading the Gospel—"that they who share with others shall also benefit and be blessed." So, in his honor, all farm animals are given extra rations. Early feeding and plenty of it indicates that a prosperous

88

Making Christmas cookies is a favorite pastime in Sweden. *Courtesy Swedish National Travel Office.*

Making the Christmas *goot* from straw is a significant part of Swedish Christmas. *Courtesy Swedish National Travel Office.*

Christmas decorations in Stockholm. *Courtesy Swedish National Travel Office.*

harvest has been enjoyed and that food and drink for the coming year will be plentiful. It is a day of carol singing, with all who participate enjoying the hospitality of friends and neighbors.

On Twelfth Night the so-called Star Boys make their appearance—especially in small communities. Youngsters dress up in strange costumes, often representing Biblical characters, among them, Judas with his money-bag. All carry large, transparent paper stars, mounted on poles, with lighted candles inside. They go from house to house, singing hymns and folk songs of ancient origin, some of which relate to the visit of the Wise Men from the East. These performances have much of the naïve charm of the medieval miracle plays.

A week later, on January 13th—St. Knut's day—the Yule-tide comes to a fitting close. (King Canute, who ruled the country a thousand years ago, had decreed that feasting at this season should last for twenty days.) As the day passes, the tree is lighted for the last time before it is dismantled, and the children sing:

> The twentieth day, King Knut did rule
> Would end the festival of Yule.

Switzerland

If Switzerland had contributed nothing more to the Christmas joy of the world than her delightful music boxes, the wonderful mechanical toys, and the fanciful cookies enjoyed by all ages, this small nation would have left her imprint permanently in the realm of Christmas lore. Of all the delightful gifts to receive at Christmas, few can rival in charm and sheer pleasure the quaint Swiss music boxes so artfully contrived and so melodious in tone. It was a Swiss watchmaker, Pierre Jaquet-Droz, who created some of the most ingenious mechanical toys ever made. They are treasures, indeed, and the stories about them rival the tales of Hans Christian Andersen and the Brothers Grimm.

In Zurich, housewives make cookies from flour and honey, known as *tirggel,* which are wonders of the culinary art. These are of German origin and were used as sacrificial cakes in pre-Christmas times. While there are dozens of kinds of cookies linked with various nations and all have some special kind of appeal in flavor, ingredients, or appearance, the *tirggel* with its long lineage, made from superbly carved wooden molds, is edible sculpture at its best. Christmas subjects are popular as motifs for this holiday delicacy and so, too, are figures of Switzerland's beloved William Tell.

In a most extraordinary way, bells carry the message of Christmas in Zurich; and in literally every village and town throughout this Alpine paradise the mellow tones of the crook-necked Alpine horns, the familiar sound of cowbells, the joyous notes of sleigh bells, and the deep resounding ring of church bells that echo through the snow-covered valleys breaking the stillness of the air make an unforgettable kind of music quite unlike that produced by any other musical

90

Fair Warning: Although Swiss children begin to celebrate Christmas early (on December 6th, in honor of St. Nicholas Day), they don't receive their presents until Christmas Eve. These children participating in one of the St. Nicholas Day parades held throughout Switzerland noisily remind their parents that there are just nineteen shopping days left until Christmas. *Courtesy Swiss Information Service.*

The Picture Hats of Urnaesch. Many weeks before the year comes to an end, youths (and grown men, too) in the village of Urnaesch in the Canton of Appenzell arrange to go Santa Clausing together. Early on New Year's Eve, they set out on their rounds as Santas-with-bells-on, some of the boys masquerading as females. On the huge headpieces affected by the "ladies," almost any subject taken from the peasants' daily life may be portrayed: the neat farmhouses, the Alpine landscape, or perhaps, as in our picture, the springtime procession to the Upland pastures. With a distinctive hopscotch gait, the revelers proceed from farmyard to farmyard, offered refreshments as they go. When evening falls, they all gravitate to the "Valley," a district of Urnaesch, where the after-dark frolicking begins. *Courtesy Swiss Information Service.*

instrument. By radio, television, and skillful recording, these sweet sounds have been carried around the world. Every nation has its bells and bell towers, but there is something truly wondrous about the ringing of the bells in Switzerland, so close to the clouds.

Christmas as enjoyed in Switzerland is colored by the customs of four distinct linguistic regions—German, French, Italian, and Romanche or Swiss. To a large extent, the populace in these segments of the country adhere closely to their individual racial heritage in observing and enjoying their own folklore. For example, in the section where German is spoken, the traditions are distinctly German and Austrian. Since Switzerland is a country of small communities rather than of large cities, many of the ancient rural folkways remain.

Here, as elsewhere in Europe, the influences of pre-Christian myths as regards crops and weather are conspicuous. As W. R. Halliday, noted English folklore scholar, has expressed it: "Myths represent the answer given by the human imagination to the problems of how things came to be." They are, in a sense, the prototypes of science. In like manner, legends are a kind of primitive history. Thus, in a country like Switzerland which has a distinct international flavor, the beliefs and notions of earlier generations, still observed and remembered, have a kind of pristine beauty that makes the story of folklore easy to understand, to enjoy, and to appreciate.

Santa Claus plays a much smaller role at Christmas in Switzerland than he does in the United States of America. In the German- and French-speaking parts of the country, gifts are brought by the *Christkindli,* the Christ Child, "a beautiful, radiant and angel-like being with wings, dressed in white, who carries a magic wand and wears a shining crown." According to popular belief, he represents Christ as a child, and he is often connected with an angel bearing a light or a star, just as an angel heralded the birth of Christ at Bethlehem. The manger setting, usually placed at the foot of the Christmas tree, is an ever-present reminder of his presence in the holiday activities. On the other hand, the *Christkindli* has some of the attributes of a sprite, as suggested by the wand and the wings which can be linked to pre-Christian beliefs, and there are those who suggest that he may stem from the pagan custom of representing the New Year as a radiant and beautiful child.

On Christmas Eve, parents decorate the tree and wrap the presents in secrecy. Despite the fact that practically every home in Switzerland is equipped with electricity, real candles are frequently used. Decorations include gold and silver garlands, multicolored blown-glass ornaments, cookies and sweets in gay wrappings, and oranges, apples, and nuts, particularly in the country. As a rule, there is a star—the Star of Bethlehem—on the top of the tree, or sometimes it is an image of the *Christkindli*. Christmas poems are recited before the gifts are distributed and the whole family gathers around the tree for a sing. In the French-speaking section of Switzerland, presents are exchanged on New Year's Day.

In all of Switzerland, it is customary for all who are able to attend church. In the mountain villages, this is a special occasion, and sometimes the only day in the year when the entire community—men, women, and children—get together, all dressed in their very best clothes. As in other countries, this is the day when family disputes sometimes are settled by public reconciliations. The

92

The St. Nicks of Kuessnacht on the Eve of St. Nicholas Day. The village of Kuessnacht, at the foot of the Rigi, resounds to the ear-splitting din of bells big and little, and of horns, trumpets, and whips. Responsible for the commotion are the masqueraders, who draw attention to themselves in this fashion. They escort more sedate Nicholases, such as those pictured here, who are enshrouded in long white shirts and beards. On their heads they support mitre-shaped lanterns over three feet high. With their elaborate perforations depicting religious figures, stars, palm branches, crosses, etc., the candlelit lanterns are an enchanting sight as they pass by in the darkness. The bearers execute ten dance steps forward, turning round and round many times with their lanterns. Then they turn to their followers, saluting them with a deep genuflection.

spirit of assembly is apparent everywhere as the farmers and mountaineers make their way down from the remote valleys and distant parts of the mountains which are generally covered with snow. They travel on foot, on skis, or on sleds, and there are those who have their sleighs drawn by horses. Harnesses are handsomely decorated and hung with little bells which create a melodious tinkling effect that adds greatly to the charm and atmosphere of the great day.

The St. Nicholas tradition in Switzerland is represented in several ways. Father Christmas, as he is called, and his wife Lucy (representing St. Lucy whose feast is on December 13th) participate in the distribution of gifts. Attired in what may be referred to as Santa Claus garb complete with white whiskers and a jolly red face, Father Christmas distributes gifts to the boys. Lucy, wearing a round cap over her long braids, a laced bodice, and a silk apron, looks after the needs of the girls.

In the heart of Switzerland, St. Nicholas lives on in a most realistic manner. Each year his impersonator dresses in the traditional bishop's garb complete with crook or crosier, as this type of ornamental staff is correctly called. His escorts are men in black hoods, carrying switches and burlap bags. The purpose of the switches needs no explanation and the burlap bags, it may be said, contain the candy, fruit, and nuts. As he makes his way about, the children's friend and hero is accompanied by bands of youngsters who carry enormous iron or brass bells which they ring with great enthusiasm. In Zurich they call him *Samichlaus,* and there, as elsewhere, he visits homes as well as schools and is sometimes accompanied by a donkey.

The Christmas story as recorded in the Bible, in all its simplicity and beauty and without the trappings of legend and folklore, is very much a part of Swiss family tradition. In this small nation where many Christian sects live in harmony, with the utmost concern for good government, spotless surroundings, and the importance of education, the account of Christ's birth is read aloud to the family on Christmas Eve.

Many unusual customs associated with farm life are still enjoyed. On Christmas Eve, either mother or grandmother searches for the best onion to be found in the vegetable closet. The onion is cut in two parts, twelve layers are peeled off, one for each of the twelve months of the year, and each is filled with salt. The following morning the family can tell by looking at the peelings which months will be dry and which will be rainy since those that have dry salt signify fair weather.

Wales

In this small country, the names of many of whose villages are not easy for us to pronounce, we find many quaint folkways to which the Welsh have clung for generations. Their contribution to Christmas lore is summed up briefly in good singing and good eating. The annual carol sings, known as *Eisteddfoddes,* are not carried on merely in the spirit of good fellowship—rather, they are keenly competitive. Thousands of voices are represented in the trained choirs which gather each year in various communities to sing of Christmas. The contests conducted to find the best music for the words of a new song are full of spirit, because the song, once accepted, will be sung everywhere the following year. Thus, the musical heritage of Wales is alive and growing.

For centuries, many strange associations have been linked with animals, particularly in countries of large rural populations. A kind of burlesque hobby horse was known in Wales called the *Mari Llwyd.* Each year someone in the village, concealed in white, would roam the community, carrying a horse's skull decorated with ribbons which was held aloft on a long pole. The skull was so arranged as to have movable jaws, and this weird creature went about biting everyone whom he met. Once held captive by the *Mari Llwyd,* the only means of release was to pay a fine.

Carol singing has been exceedingly popular in Wales for generations. A century ago, this small nation outranked England in the quality and the excellence of its Christmas music. Often, carols were sung to the accompaniment of the harp. At *Plygain* (dawn service or the crowing of the cock) held at four o'clock on Christmas Morning, it was common practice for the young men in some villages to escort the rector with lighted torches from his house to the church. After the service, which consisted of a sermon and the singing of hymns until daybreak, the torches were relighted and the procession returned to the rectory. Today, this custom is sometimes observed on New Year's morning, but it has long ceased to be a part of the Christmas service.

Housewives pride themselves in making plum puddings that keep moist for several years, and it would not be *Nadolig* (Christmas) without a taffy-pull. Early in the nineteenth century, the members of two Welsh parishes gathered on Christmas Day for a game of football, and the vivid account of this game which is on record indicates that football was obviously a sport of prime importance at the time and that it was a matter of great pride to the members of the parish who retained the ball.

Before dawn, on New Year's Day, children made a practice of carrying about a jug of water which had been freshly drawn from a nearby well. Carrying a sprig of boxwood or some other kind of everygreen, they roamed the village, singing and sprinkling all whom they met, wishing them the compliments of the season. In paying their respects to those who were not yet awake, they knocked on doors to rouse friends and neighbors and serenaded them with the verses of an ancient song known as the "new water" carol.

Latin America

Merry Christmas is *Feliz Navidad* in the Spanish-speaking nations of Latin America, but it is *Bom Natal* if you live in big Brazil where the language is Portuguese, or *Joyeuse Noël* if your home is on the hot tropical island of Haiti.

In most, but not all, of these neighboring countries, Christmas comes in the hottest time of year. Those who live in the Northern Hemisphere instinctively associate Christmas with a snow-covered landscape rather than its true setting, which is tropical and much more like that of Latin America. Then, too, the spirit of Christmas south of the Rio Grande is colored by great religious devotion on the one hand and carnival-like gaiety on the other. This unusual blend of emotion springs from a cultural background that is conspicuously Spanish and Portuguese, differing in many ways from the (to us) more familiar folkways of the British, the Scandinavian, and the Slavic countries.

Schools close at the end of November for a vacation that lasts until the first of February. During this leisurely summer siesta, there are five holidays. These are the Feast of Purissima or the Immaculate Conception on December 8th, Nochebuena (Christmas Eve), Christmas Day, Holy Innocents' Day (December 28th), and the Feast of the Three Kings on January 6th.

In addition to colorful religious services, fiestas held at this time of year are enhanced by an abundance of local customs and traditions as well as those of the Old World. Quantities of fresh flowers embellish the *nacimientos* (crib scenes) in Costa Rica and elsewhere. Church services are often held in the open and Christmas dinner may be served in the garden. Dances like the *bambuco* in Colombia, the *joropo* in Venezuela, the *meringue* in the Caribbean, and the *cueca* in Chile usher in the season with a flourish. Roast pig with all the trimmings is part of the Christmas feast in many places. In various parts of Colombia, the ceremony of killing and cooking the pig reminds us of a gala barbecue. Moreover, this is the time for horse races, bullfights, parades, displays of fireworks, plays, intricate tribal dances, boating excursions, and other diversions quite different from those enjoyed in colder parts of the world.

96

Some of the seasonal traditions are common to all the nations, but many have distinctive national or regional customs of their own. For example, the Feast of Purissima is generally considered a wholly religious day, with special Masses in the churches, but some nations celebrate it with public processions in the evening accompanied by plenty of firecrackers and Roman candles to ensure both noise and light.

The preparation for Christmas Eve, however, is the same everywhere. All families, rich or poor, build a manger scene. It may be only a few inches square (or smaller in El Salvador, famous for its exquisite minuscule figurines) or big enough to fill an entire patio or room. Whether it is called a *portal* as in Costa Rica, a *pesebre* as in Colombia, or a *nacimiento* as in most other countries, it is sure to be the center of family life during the holiday season. The making of the manger is a family project, with something new added every day. The traditional figures of the Holy Family, the shepherds, the angels, and the Wise Men are always the same, but local color is provided by innovations ranging from llamas to motorbikes, from mermaids to marimba players.

As in Spain, the midnight service on Christmas Eve in churches throughout Latin America is known as *Missa de Gallo,* the Mass of the Rooster, since it commemorates the only time when the cock crowed at midnight—in Bethlehem, a long time ago. Despite the hour, this is the time when boys in Lima, Peru, and other places take advantage of the occasion to imitate the crow of the cock, the bray of the donkey, and the mooing of the cow, using whistles and rattles to render their efforts more dramatic.

Christmas Eve is more important than Christmas Day in many parts of Latin America. It is then that the Christ Child is placed in the crib and familiar *villancicos* (carols) are heard. The Peruvians sing *"Esta noche es la Noche buena y no es la noche de dormir"* (This night is the Good Night and not a night to sleep), and prove it by staying up for midnight Mass, after which they return for a heavy *cena,* or meal, usually of tamales.

In Mexico, groups of all ages form *posadas* (processions) and go from house to house asking for entrance, as they reenact the Holy Family's search for shelter. This custom takes the form of *trullas* in Puerto Rico, where guitar-playing caballeros, their señoritas mounted pillion behind them, ride horseback from farm to farm through the soft tropical night, caroling as they go. Everywhere, the carols, known as *aguinaldos* and *villancicos,* are sung to the accompaniment of strumming guitars, or to the click of maracas, or to the sweet soft notes of the harp, or to the haunting sounds of the *rondadores* (bamboo shepherds' pipes).

In the sturdy little Central American country of Costa Rica, Christmas is an orchidaceous holiday. On the high cool plains of the *paramo,* the trees are hung so thickly with all kinds of bromeliads and orchids that it is possible to trace the route of the wind by the clusters of blossoms.

The charming, clean capital of San José has a carnival air from December 15th to Christmas Day. Kiosks appear near the big market and in any open space available where people buy colored sawdust and moss for the *portals.* Inexpensive toys, many hand-made, are for sale, especially the small whistles that are the delight of younger children who greet the dawn of Christmas Day with a cacophony of shrill sounds. Stores are open every night until ten-thirty,

97

In Guatemala it would not be Christmas without the colored sawdust sold in the markets for use in the *nacimientos* which are set up in every home in tribute to the Christ Child. *Courtesy Mary Scrimshaw.*

Even youngsters help make trinkets for the Christmas markets in Mexico.

Red tulip-shaped lanterns add a dramatic note to the Christmas Eve processions in Oaxaca, Mexico, where a figure of the Christ Child is carried to church with great ceremony. *Courtesy Virginia C. Shattuck.*

The Christmas parade in the Bahama Islands.

and shopping becomes a gay *paseo* as friends shower each other with confetti on Avendo Central.

In many sections of South America, gift-giving used to be linked entirely with Epiphany, since those of Spanish and Portuguese origin cling to the old tradition of the Wise Men. It has long been their cherished belief that the Magi traveled through those countries on their way to Bethlehem. On the other hand, Santa Claus or Papa Noël and the Christmas tree are becoming better known each year.

Holy Innocents' Day, December 28th, is observed in hilarious fashion—rather like a combination of April Fool's Day and Halloween. Like the practice of barring the schoolmaster and the nonsense revolving around the Lord of Misrule, children run the gamut of pranks and practical jokes. They are largely aided by their parents, who join in the antics of the day with great zest.

In Costa Rica, after playing a joke on someone you shout, *"Paso por inocencia comiendo pan caliente!"* Practical jokers telephone and make announcements like "This is the Police Department. You are under arrest for murder." Newspapers in Chile use headlines to play jokes on their readers—in Santiago it was announced that Elvis Presley was marrying a Chilean actress in Viña del Mar. Hundreds of people flocked to Viña and hovered around the churches in vain. Another tall story was the announcement that a flying saucer had landed. In Colombia, a favorite device for deceiving the innocent is to serve delicious-looking doughnuts strongly flavored with mustard. The old expression *ponga cuidado* (if you lend money on this day you won't be paid back), is often heard on December 28th.

However, in Haiti no jokes are played. This is *the* day for young children. Even the tiniest members of the family are carried to church for a special service which includes a blessing and the presentation of a medal, a little statue, or a piece of candy. Each child is then allowed to kiss the figure of the Christ Child which is displayed with great ceremony. This is also a popular day to give children's parties.

Quaint old folkways found in certain parts of Latin America, like those elsewhere in the world, are being modified to contemporary life. Traditions with their roots and origins in Italy, France, Holland, Great Britain, and the United States as well as Spain and Portugal, have been transplanted. However, because of early colonization by the Spanish and the Portuguese, overtones of these two cultures are naturally predominant. Then, too, the influence of the native Indians whose pre-Christian rites were adapted to Christian ways is apparent everywhere. Even the indomitable spirit and influence of Dickens is easily recognized in some present-day Christmas customs.

A naïve kind of beauty and sentiment permeates many of the folk customs observed in Central and South America. While the influence of North America is obvious (as are ancient practices and new ones, too, introduced from Europe), there is also present a delightful childlike sense of devotion, awe, and wonder in the observance of Christmas among the various Indian tribes. The pomp, the pageantry, and the ritual of the Roman Catholic churches have warm appeal for many of them. In like manner, the various Protestant churches have also inaugurated traditions and practices whose influence is apparent on every side.

99

Yet, in the over-all picture, the folkways of the Indians stand out conspicuously. Theirs is a simple way of life, as ranch workers, miners, and farmers, and their culture is of very ancient origin. Tribal dances, a love of costumes, historic rites linked with crops, ceremonial foods, and other manifestations of primitive culture give their Christmas a unique appeal. Missionaries of many faiths, keenly aware of the importance of tribal lore, have encouraged its continuance, and it remains today in the countries of Latin America a strong link with the traditions of bygone centuries.

Brazil

In many parts of Brazil, Christmas comes at the hottest time of year. It is also vacation time from school and the season for boating, picnics, and other pleasant summer diversions. In São Paulo, where the influence of Europe and the United States is conspicuous, shop windows are beautifully decorated, with prizes offered for the best displays. Santa Claus and his many helpers, decked out in their typical winter costumes, walk about the streets giving small gifts to the children. Families who are financially able invite a child from a local orphanage to spend Christmas week as a guest in their homes, and, in most instances, they continue their interest in the child's welfare after he returns to the orphanage. (In Rio, the children assemble at the arena to give Papa Noël a warm reception. He arrives by helicopter and distributes gifts, such as water pistols, balloons, whistles, and similar toys.)

The making of *pesebres* is a favorite pastime, and these are often amusing in appearance because there is no attempt to choose figures of appropriate sizes to give the effect of pleasing scale. Bright-colored sawdust is especially popular for use in making the *pesebre*. Each day, beginning with Christmas, the figures of the Three Kings are moved forward a little to symbolize their journey from the East to Bethlehem. The loudest firecrackers are kept until Epiphany, when they are set off to indicate the end of the Christmas season.

On Christmas Eve, the tree is seen for the first time, having been decorated behind locked doors. As in Europe, it is lighted with candles, and everyone sings carols. Children put out their shoes for Papa Noël to fill. Before midnight Mass, many families often set the table for the *cena,* complete with all the food for the meal, so that the Holy Family may come in and eat, if they wish, while the family is in church. The *cena* includes turkey, fish, champagne, and many delicacies. The last candle of the Advent wreath is lighted and the Christ Child is placed in his crib in the *pesebre*. All-night gaiety prevails in communities large and small, and the air is filled with the sound of bells, happy voices, and firecrackers.

Louis Agassiz, noted nineteenth-century naturalist, and his wife who visited Brazil nearly a century ago, recorded many of the colorful customs which they observed. In their diary for Christmas Day we read: "At nightfall, from the settlements at Hyanuary, two illuminated canoes come across the river to

100

Manaos; one bearing the figure of Our Lady, the other of Saint Rosalia. They look very brilliant as they come towards the shore, all the light concentrated about the figures carried erect in the prows. On landing, the Indians, many of whom have come to the city in advance, form a procession—the women dressed in white, and with flowers in their hair, the men carrying torches or candles; and they follow the sacred images, which are borne under a canopy in front of the procession, to the church, where they are deposited, and remain during Christmas week. We entered with them, and saw the kneeling, dusky congregation, and the two saints,—one a wooden coarsely painted image of the Virgin, the other a gayly dressed doll,—placed on a small altar, where was also a figure of the infant Jesus, surrounded by flowers."

On Christmas Day, the children serve breakfast to their parents in bed, but, as one might expect, the food is rather poorly prepared since they are more eager to find the presents which Papa Noël has hidden all over the house than to play host to their elders. Surprisingly enough, the most popular dessert on this special day is canned peaches from California, topped with whipped cream. In the afternoon, while the children play with their toys, their parents chat and sometimes dance. Fireworks in the evening bring the great day to a close. Holiday decorations include eucalyptus leaves and many kinds of red flowers.

Chile

In the small town of Andacollo, Chile, Christmas is observed in a most charming and unusual manner. In the days of Inca domination, this community became famous for streams of gold that floated out of the riverbed. However, the gold meant little to the natives since it became the property of the emperor. Tradition has it that one of the native Indians, named Collo, had a dream in which an angel appeared to him urging him to "go to the hills, for wealth and happiness await you." He went, and, while he was making his way through the brush, his hatchet struck a strange object. He excavated and unearthed a statue of the Virgin, three feet tall, for which he made a shrine in his hut. Soon the natives began to worship before the figure and Collo became her guardian.

Each year, thousands of people come to Andacollo during the Christmas fiesta to pay tribute to the Virgin in a highly dramatic ceremony which includes a procession, a ritual, and a series of native dances. The performers dress themselves in colorful costumes and the Virgin is placed on a platform surrounded by roses. Dressed in a white robe embroidered with gold, the statue is arrayed with all the precious trappings of royalty and her crown and that of the Christ Child are made of precious stones. Thus, the Virgin del Rosario has greatly enriched the Christmas traditions of this remote community and the tribute paid her by the local people is known today over a large part of the world.

Here, as in other parts of South America, Christmas comes at the hottest time of the year and is the beginning of vacation time. Santa Claus, who is called *Viejo Pascuero,* travels through the sky with his reindeer, entering each home

101

through a window, but it is the belief of the children that he will not visit unless they are asleep when he arrives. But, like children in other parts of the world, they write letters to him and then put building blocks under their pillows to keep awake so that they can catch a glimpse of Santa.

Christmas bread, called *pan de pasqua,* made in a round loaf and filled with candied fruit, is a favorite for breakfast on Christmas morning. For the festive dinner, most families are sure to have *azuela de ave* (chicken soup made with potatoes, onions, and corn on the cob). A curious small, long-handled fork is used for eating the corn. Many of the holiday customs observed in Chile are typical of those popular in other South American countries.

Colombia

The "Yankees of Colombia," as the independent, progressive residents of the northwestern state of Antioquia are often referred to, have Christmas customs that center largely around their country homes. In this superbly beautiful section of the Andes, the prosperous capital of Medellin towers five thousand feet above the sea and is encircled by still higher mountains. Here the Medellinenses build their delightful haciendas, smothering porches and patios in bougainvillea, jasmine, roses, and orchids. From these colorful bowers they can look down through space into the city and be grateful that they live in Antioquia—a form of smugness not unknown in New England and certain other parts of our country.

As Katharine Van Etten Lyford describes it, the three-week period beginning on December 15th and extending to January 6th is just one *marrano asado* (barbecue) after another.

In the clean mountain air people grow hungry, so on hand is a mountain of delicious snacks and plenty of soft and hard drinks to wash them down. Also, there is plenty of music supplied by phonograph records. Musicians often play folk music on the *bambuco,* or possibly a local *conjunto* or guitar, and the *maracas.* Although everyone sings familiar songs, there is little if any dancing.

"At last it is time to eat the pig, the fragrance of which has been tantalizing appetites for hours. By now it may be the middle of the afternoon or later and everyone promptly eats too much and thoroughly enjoys doing so. Along with the roast pork there are *arepas* (flat corn meal cakes) in which I have never been able to detect the slightest flavor but they are greatly relished by Antioquians and crisp, delicious fried *bunuelos* (the Colombian version of doughnuts)."

Another Christmas custom, traditional only in Antioquia, is the sending up of the *globo,* a huge balloon made of of colored paper. The whole family takes part in making it, using a special kind of thin, bright-colored *papel de globo* (balloon paper) which is cut into sixteen triangular pieces. When glued together, the balloon stands four or five feet high. Sometimes the balloons are made in even larger sizes. At the base is a ring of wire to which are fastened rags dipped in gasoline. It takes eight children to hold out the sides of the balloon so that air

can inflate it, but this is no problem since families in Antioquia are always large. (They "begin with five children" and often run to twelve or fifteen.) Since the final handling of the balloon involves dangerous manipulation, this is usually taken over by the father of the family. When a match is applied to the rags, he holds the *globo* as high in the air as possible and turns around solemnly three times as he releases it into the air. *Globos* are not allowed in the sugar-cane country because of the danger of fire, and for the same reason they are illegal in towns and cities. Although the use of these balloons is in fact illegal throughout the country, they are so much a part of the Christmas observance that no one is prosecuted for carrying on this picturesque tradition.

Costa Rica

Bringing in the orchids is one of the many pleasant customs that mark the beginning of the Christmas season in Costa Rica. This is the time of year for a special trip to the high *paramo* to gather them. Orchids grow so abundantly on the trees that the direction of the breeze can be determined from the way in which the blooms cluster along the branches, as mentioned before. Often, small logs are gathered from the woods and hollowed out to make containers in which to arrange the brilliantly colored blooms, and when candles are added the result is a holiday centerpiece of great charm and beauty.

But more important is the manner in which the manger scenes (or *portals*) are decorated, using all the bounty of nature. Flowers, fruits, and foliage in great profusion are gathered to glorify del Niño (the Christ Child) on his birthday. Framed with richly textured mosses, forming a velvety green background for the jewel-like orchids, the *portal* becomes a kind of rococo replica of the ornate shrines seen in Old World churches. The making of these elaborate manger settings has long been an important part of the Christmas tradition in Costa Rica. Often they are large panoramas, reminiscent of Bethlehem as the Costa Ricans imagine it, and may occupy an entire room. As friends go from house to house to see what their neighbors have accomplished, a pleasant kind of rivalry develops and families vie with one another in adding touches of novelty and originality to their handiwork. Mountains, lakes, and forests dot the highly imaginative landscape which is peopled with tiny figures both religious and secular. Each year, more figures are added—sometimes a new angel, another lamb or two, or some appropriate trinket the family thinks will delight del Niño. At midnight Mass, his image is taken from the *portal* in the church and carried down the aisle by the priest for the adoration of the worshippers.

According to Costa Rican tradition, it is del Niño who brings the children their gifts, but in recent years Santa Claus has appeared on the scene from the United States and parents delight in imitating the sound of reindeer hoofs on Christmas Eve to inform their children that Santa is arriving.

Also of recent origin in Costa Rica is the Christmas tree. Usually of native pine, it is topped with a scroll reading *Gloria in Excelsis Deo* and is hung with

103

all manner of bright ornaments. The tree often serves as a setting for the *portal*, but, at best, it is of secondary importance. Fresh fruits arranged in a basket, especially tropical kinds which are aromatic and spicy, are placed on a table near the *portal* to symbolize the gifts of the Wise Men. *Coronitas* (wreaths) made of cypress, ornamented with red coffee berries, are hung in the windows.

In every city and town, small stalls or kiosks are erected to sell toys, fire-crackers, cookies, candy, pinecones, moss, orchids, and colored sawdust for use in the *portals*. Christmas shopping in San José has a true fiesta flair as folks stroll through the streets in the evening, tossing confetti at their friends when they stop to make a purchase or enjoy light refreshments.

A visit to grandmother is a special Christmas event for the children since it provides an opportunity for a party in front of the *portal* with carols to the accompaniment of the harp and the guitar. The village priest is on hand to lead the family in the recitation of the rosary followed by *El Tedel Niño* (the Child's tea) which consists of hot chocolate, *incamelado* (a cinnamon cake), *illustrados* (cookies with shiny frosting), hot bread, and other good things to eat. The supper served following midnight Mass includes tamales stuffed with chicken, olives, rice, and other ingredients, all colored with red chili.

Ecuador

Christmas as celebrated on a ranch in Ecuador is not too far removed in spirit from the manner in which it is observed in the United States or in many parts of Europe. As Katharine Van Etten Lyford reminds us in her vivid account, *Christmas on the Hacienda,* only the setting and the weather differ. Under summer skies, in an atmosphere that is truly tropical, the Indians deck themselves in their brightest clothes. Even their llamas wear bells and colorful blankets. The Indians come to the ranches of their employers for the great day, carrying as gifts to the Christ Child the best they have to offer.

The *pesebre*, or manger setting, usually arranged in a large wooden box lined with blue paper, has a prominent place near the entrance hall of the *hacienda*. The Bethlehem skyline painted on the blue paper serves as a background for paper hills, white sand roads, mossy mounds, mirror lakes and rivers, and other prominent landscape features. The Holy Family and all the traditional figures, dolls made of bread dough portraying the Indian children garbed in their dance costumes, sheep, llamas, and a variety of curiosities such as paper angels and stars, give life to the setting.

"Shepherds herd tiny sheep across the mirror stream and the new llamas stalk their stiff-legged way down the paper mountains. Indian children dance on the sandy road toward the cave of the Holy Family which is guarded on one side by the Wise Men and on the other by a bread dough cow and a new burro."

The Indians make their way down the mountain to the *hacienda,* calling to one another across the deep valleys with their *bocinas,* tremendous six-foot-long horns. They are led by a boy and a girl dressed in bright feathered costumes, their faces colored red and blue, who act as heralds for the procession.

"A second *bocina* gives answer, then a third and a fourth from other cloud-hung peaks. Soon shepherds' pipes and dulcimers blend their minor cadences in traditional Quechuan chants until the hills and valleys echo and re-echo with melodies. Lights prick the overhanging clouds and chains of firefly lanterns loop the mountain slopes as the Indians wend their way down steep trails to merge on the lower hillsides in the traditional Christmas procession to the *hacienda*.

"Indian men, dressed in their gayest ponchos and freshly chalked woolen hats, are followed by their wives, plump ballerinas with short, full skirts belled out over petticoats of purple, orange and green. Fastened to their mothers' shoulders with striped shawls, chubby dark-skinned babies gaze round-eyed at the lively scene about them.

"Even the llamas seem to have caught the holiday spirit. Their customary look of disdain changes to one of smug self-satisfaction as they stretch their long, bell-trimmed necks or shake their purple saddle cloths fringed with mirrors and coins, to make them jingle."

When they have unloaded their goods and tethered their llamas, the Indians follow the heralds up the front steps of the *hacienda* to the manger, before which the figure of the Christ Child has been placed on a table to receive his gifts.

As the little heralds slip away, the older Indians surge forward to see the Babe of Bethlehem and to present their gifts. Soon table and floor are piled high with eggs, oranges, sugarcane, wool, live hens, dead rabbits, and still more eggs. Everything from gourds to guinea pigs is offered with the same reverence as were the gold, frankincense, and myrrh of old. Then the children present their gifts, recite pretty speeches to the Child Jesus, and ask his blessing for their families, their llamas, the other *animales,* and their crops.

Once the Indians have looked their fill at the manger, they drift back into the patio. Forming a huge circle under the blossomed apple trees, they chant ancient Quechuan songs with a haunting, strange kind of sadness. Yet the words are simple, devout and joyous:

> My sweet Jesus,
> My tiny Loved One,
> Come to my soul, Little One,
> Come, don't wait too long.
>
> Come, shepherds,
> Come, shepherds,
> Come and adore
> The King of Heaven
> Who is born today.

And as they sing the people dance in a long circling line, weaving a living wreath of vivid blues, reds, and purples in the bright tropic sunshine.

Later, a change of mood occurs as all ages scramble in great merriment for the coins tossed by the ranch owner's family. Then comes the distribution of gifts. There are shirts for women and girls; cookies and candy for everyone.

The festive meal includes roast lamb, baked potatoes, and brown-sugar bread, freshly baked for the occasion. It takes considerable planning and estimating to provide enough food for all the guests as well as an ample supply to take home, for it is as much the custom as dancing and singing for this Indian tribe to bring great clay *ollas* (jars) to the feast to gather up the leftovers which they carry away to enjoy at home.

105

Guatemala

In this Central American country, Christmas means tortoiseshell drums to provide the special offbeat rhythm heard only during these holidays. It also means thousands of *farolitos* (gaily painted tin lanterns lighted with candles) which are carried through the streets in the *posada* processions each night for nine days before Christmas. Everywhere, thousands of flaming bushes are blooming, bent to the ground with brilliant poinsettia blossoms.

Before the Christmas holidays start, there is another December holiday called El Dia de Guadalupe (the Day of Guadalupe). This celebration, held on December 8th, honors the beloved bronze-skinned Virgin of Guadalupe, who first appeared to a little Indian boy named Santiago a long time ago and later became the patron of Mexico and of all Indians.

In Guatemala City, children prepare for this fiesta with great delight. Each and every one dresses in traditional Indian costume, complete even to the minutest detail. For days before the feast, the local markets sell miniature *cacastes* (baskets or frames). These are exact replicas of the kind the Guatemalan Indians use for carrying produce. The boys' *cacastes* are filled with miniature chickens, vegetables, sausages, eggs, and other foods, while the girls carry small water jars on their heads or balance baskets of tortillas in similar fashion, covered with bright-colored cloth.

Along the streets near the Church of Guadalupe, stalls are set up where crisp, delectable *bunelos* (fritters) made with honey are fried and the hot spicy *batidos* (a drink flavored with ginger and *achiote*) is served in gaily painted *jicaras* (gourds). The hard enamel finish on these artistic *jicaras* gives them a high gloss, the result of a secret process that preserves the colors from fading.

A great parade is held on this important feast day and along the route elaborate settings for photographs are staged. Thus, the costumed children can have their pictures taken against such backgrounds as a bamboo Indian hut, the making of tortillas, the playing of the marimba, or some other typical Indian activity. Every parading child and his proud parents insist on a photographic memento of El Dia de Guadalupe. During the day there are firecrackers, and also at night when the parents dress up in Indian costumes to attend parties or dances at private homes and clubs.

Nine days before Christmas the *posadas* begin. For the most part, these are similar to the Mexican *posadas,* but they do have some distinct features of their own. On the ninth day before Christmas, it is customary for many families in Guatemala to place statues of Mary and Joseph on a large platform and invite their friends to join them for the evening *posada*. The platform is carried through the dark streets on the shoulders of two men, accompanied by members of the family and as many as twenty or thirty friends. As they march along, one of the paraders plays the turtle drum and the *ticka, ticka, too, ticka, ticka, too* beat (used only for Christmas *posadas*) can be heard for blocks. All the paraders carry lighted *farolitos* of a special kind and usually some of the group have a supply of firecrackers which they set off en route.

Arriving at the home of a friend (who actually expects them), they sing the

106

widely known Christmas carol asking for shelter (enacting the episode of Joseph and Mary arriving in Bethlehem). The family inside the house (behind a closed door) refuses to let them enter, asking who they are and why such strangers should be invited in. The carol continues with questions and answers until the outside serenaders explain that they are Joseph and Mary. At this announcement the family sings, "Open the door and let them in." Then the members of the *posada* enter, carrying the figures of Joseph and Mary to a *nacimiento* which has previously been made ready to receive the Holy Family. At this time both family and guests join in reciting the Rosary and the novena for the day. After this ceremony, hot punch and tamales are served. Then the guests dance to the music of the marimbas.

The next evening, the family which has sheltered the statues of Joseph and Mary overnight remove them from the *nacimiento,* gather their friends, and start their own *posada.* Thus, the figures of the Virgin and Joseph visit nine homes, carried each time by *posadas* of twenty or thirty people from house to house. On Christmas Eve, the *posada* ends at a home large enough to invite all the people who have taken part in the nightly processions.

This is the time when the figure of the Christ Child is added to the *nacimiento.* Family and friends assemble in a dark room carrying lighted candles and some type of noisemaker or rattle. One member holds a large silver tray mounded with yards of fluffy, pastel tulle (to represent clouds) with the Christ Child resting in the center. After a procession around the patio, the group surrounds the *nacimiento* and places the Child in the crib. Children are so very fond of figures of the Babe of Bethlehem that they often insist upon having their own, with the result that many *nacimientos* are crowded with figurines of the Christ Child.

Because of the large German population in Guatemala, the Christmas tree has become traditional. Usually the presents (brought by the Christ Child) are put under the tree, and frequently the *nacimiento* is placed there too. Ornaments are likely to be from Germany, but the trees are the long-needled pine imported from the United States. On December 24th, people go to midnight Mass, then come home for the *cena* (supper). On December 25th, children get up early to see their presents and play with them. Christmas dinner is an informal affair; usually the family eats leftovers from the night before. New Year's Eve is the occasion for many parties in clubs and millions of firecrackers spark the celebration. It is on New Year's Day that the adults receive gifts—only the children get theirs at Christmas. Employers give their employees money or gifts, and some adults exchange gifts, too.

Mexico

One might think that Christmas in Mexico was spelled with a capital letter *P,* for much of the festive spirit revolves around *posadas, piñatas,* and *puestos.* As previously noted, the *posada,* which means "inn" or "place of lodging," is actually a religious procession in which Joseph's fruitless search for shelter for Mary on the way to Bethlehem is reenacted with great dramatic fervor. (Originally, this episode was part of an old Spanish Christmas play, *Los Pastores* [The Shepherds], written around the incidents relating to the birth of the Christ Child.) The *piñata* is an earthenware jar cleverly disguised as an animal, a person, or some curious object which is filled with toys and good things to eat and is meant to be broken to redeem the treasures it contains. This is accomplished by using a stick which children wield, blindfolded, in a kind of game that provides both hilarity and excitement. The *puesto* is a market stall which the Indians set up wherever there is space in order to sell the Christmas toys, rag dolls, figurines, and trinkets which they have been making for weeks.

All in all, the holiday season is a time of elaborate pageantry, fireworks, feasting, and frivolity—a blend of reverence and revelry that radiates with all the brilliance of the flaming poinsettia which blooms at Christmas in Mexico. The native name of the poinsettia is "Flower of Christmas Eve" and the legendary account of its origin bears out the appropriateness of this endearing name. As with the story of the Christmas rose its origin was a miracle. A little Mexican boy named Pablo, eager to visit the manger in the village church, was chagrined because he had no suitable gift to offer. Nonetheless, he gathered branches of green leaves from a bush that grew along the dusty road and took them to the church. The other children mocked him, but when they looked a second time a brilliant red star-shaped flower topped each branch!

The bright red, green, and white stripes of the Mexican flag seen everywhere add further glamour to the season, as do the candles of similar colors used in the *posadas* as well as for decorations in the adobes. The gleam of mellow light from lanterns and *luminarios* amid a setting of Spanish moss and evergreen boughs lends another festive touch.

Las posadas begin nine days before Christmas, commemorating the time it took Mary and Joseph to make the journey from Nazareth to Bethlehem. It may be enacted by nine families who meet at a different house each night, making of the occasion an elaborate ceremonial and social affair, or it may be carried out by a single family at home as part of the traditional Christmas ritual. However, some families observe the occasion on a single evening. In any case, the participants are divided into two groups, the pilgrims and the innkeepers. The evening begins with the rosary led by the head of the house. Then family, friends, and guests representing the pilgrims form a procession and march around the house carrying lighted candles. Usually two children take the lead, carrying figures of Joseph and Mary. Each innkeeper takes his place in one of the rooms. Moving from room to room, the pilgrims chant the Litany of Loretto as they knock at the various doors asking for shelter, but in each instance they are refused admittance. (The word *litany,* which means a humble and fervent ap-

108

These are the *santos,* elaborately decorated wooden figures, made by Puerto Rican craftsmen and greatly cherished as family heirlooms. *Courtesy Puerto Rican Information Service.*

At the Christmas Market in Oaxaca, Mexico, enormous radishes fashioned like men, women, and animals are sold along with tiny bejeweled lambs, lanterns, toys, and sweets. *Courtesy Virginia C. Shattuck.*

peal, is a form of prayer found in both the Old and the New Testaments.) The Litany of Loretto is either read or memorized and forms the basis for a simple and beautiful devotion in which all who are present may take part. Thus, in *las posadas,* these lines convey the essence of the simple drama:

> "Who knocks at my door, so late in the night?"
> "We are pilgrims, without shelter, and we want only a place to rest."
> "Go somewhere else and disturb me not again."
> "But the night is very cold. We have come from afar and we are very tired."
> "But who are you? I know you not."
> "I am Joseph of Nazareth, a carpenter, and with me is Mary, my wife, who will be the mother of the Son of God."
> "Then come into my humble home, and welcome! And may the Lord give shelter to my soul when I leave this world!"

At last, the pilgrims reach a room where an altar has been previously set up, and, having furnished proper identification, they are allowed to enter. A song of joy is heard, followed by these humble words of prayer:

> O God, who in coming to save us, didst not disdain a humble stable, grant that we may never close our hearts when thou art knocking so that we may be made worthy to be received into thy sight when our hour comes.

The altar is a Nativity scene elaborately decked with mosses, greens, and flowers—staged against a hillside setting complete with miniature houses, sheep, shepherds, an assortment of trees and other landscape features, and all the detail to give a feeling of the Bethlehem setting. The figures of Mary and Joseph are placed in the stable and the procedure is followed each night until Christmas Eve, when the Christ Child is laid in the manger.

With the ceremonial completed, refreshments are served and then comes the *piñata* party. This unique custom, brought from Spain centuries ago is also a familiar part of the Christmas observance throughout the southwestern United States, where the Spanish settled in the seventeenth century.

Usually the *piñata* is suspended from the branch of a tree. Decorated with streamers and tinsel, it is exceedingly colorful and often shows great imagination in design. Birds, fish, horses, shoes, ships, houses, men and women are typical of the shapes in which they are made. Each child is blindfolded, whirled around several times, and then given a big stick. It often requires many a whack and an equal number of "misses" before the blow is made that cracks the *piñata*. Then comes the grand scramble for the goodies, which vary from dolls to tiny carts, trinkets of every description, and, naturally, candy and fruits. (As is the custom in most countries in tropical America, the Three Kings bring the presents on January 6th.) Sometimes the *piñatas* are made in the shape of dolls beautifully dressed in elaborate and colorful costumes. It should be mentioned in passing that this quaint and charming old custom has warm appeal for all who witness it and is greatly enjoyed at Christmas in many parts of North and South America far removed from Mexico.

Visitors to Mexico at this season of the year are always fascinated by the Christmas markets. Indians of all ages from young children to aged grandparents

110

participate in the making of playthings, ornaments, and the amazing variety of trinkets which are offered for sale. Every conceivable kind of craft is represented, including weaving, carving, pottery, painting, and the allied arts. Then, too, there are *puestos* offering all sorts of good things to eat: cheeses, preserved bananas, candies, cookies made of anjonjoli seed, figs, dates, thin red peppers, nuts, and a host of sweetmeats. Having worked for weeks to produce their goods, the Indian families travel long distances from their mountain villages to the cities by truck, by donkey, or on foot in order to sell their wares. Thus, the *puestos* spring up everywhere there is space enough for even the tiniest booth— or merely a place to squat.

Virginia C. Shattuck has recorded her impressions of one of these markets and a Christmas Eve procession in a charming story which she entitles *A Christmas Fantasy:* "The Christmas market of Oaxaca is especially gay. Quantities of orchids are brought in from the hills and also many interesting air plants (epiphytes) which are used to decorate the creches. Although visitors delight in buying orchids to their hearts' content, the principal purchasers are the Indians. They buy flowers in the market and trudge hot and weary hours back to their villages to decorate their family altars. An Indian woman looking at the wilted flowers in her hand shook her head and smiled. *'No importa'*—no matter, the Virgin will understand.

"Two days before Christmas Indians were quietly putting up stands around the four sides of the plaza but little did we realize what a transformation was taking place. We had been told that these were the preparations for Radish night. By night it was another world.

"In some booths were enchanting little lambs which looked as though they were covered with tiny diamonds. Others had candy for sale in little baskets made of tissue paper and colored cellophane. They covered the tables and hung from the upper frames catching the many lights as they swayed in the breeze. Everywhere there were toys and goodies—but above all, there were the radishes. They ranged from twelve inches to two feet in length and their roots were cleverly worked into the arms and legs of men and women. One was carved as an elephant. Another was dressed as a warrior doing a plume dance. Many were wearing the handsome Tehauna costume with its elaborate lace head dress. They hung from frames which were decorated with evergreens. Lights were everywhere. Venetian lanterns as well as brighter lights showed up the radish folk as they swayed back and forth.

"The crowd was gay, orderly and friendly. I had a camera and flash bulbs but was hesitant about using them since I did not want to offend anyone. Seeing my equipment, a gentleman got up from his seat, tipped his hat and suggested that if I stood where he had been sitting, I could get a better view of the next booth. Again and again, the Indians made way for me to photograph and one salesman held a radish so that I might get a better view of it.

"On this one night in the year in the adjoining Alameda, you buy a pancake in a pottery dish, eat it with syrup and smash the plate on the cobblestones. Before the evening ended the street would be three inches deep in broken earthenware. Such a happy carnival! To prove that there was magic, the next morning the booths were gone, there was not a fragment of a broken dish and not so much as a piece of paper was on the ground.

111

"Then came Christmas Eve! Would it be anti-climax? No booths this time but there was an air of expectancy in the milling crowd. Music soon was heard from far down one of the streets and lights appeared. 'Señora, they are coming this way.' A Mexican I had never seen before wanted me to get a good photograph of the first of the Christmas Eve processions. The 'good will toward men' of the Christmas anthem was shown that evening by many kindly acts.

"On Christmas Eve in Oaxaca the candle light processions leave the churches of the *'barrios,'* or districts, circle to the plaza and, just before midnight, each returns to its own church for the Missa de Gallo, or midnight Mass.

"The first procession seemed to me the loveliest—perhaps because there was the element of surprise. It was like a river of bobbing red tulips flowing toward us. Some of the tulips were taller than others. Men, women and children were carrying the flower-shaped lanterns, each attached to the end of a reed or wand. Later, I had a chance to examine one of the lanterns. It was made of dyed bladder stretched on thin loops of bamboo and it was soft to the touch as fine silk.

"At the front of each procession was a banner telling the name of the church from which it came and somewhere near the center walked a woman carrying the Christ Child on a cushion. She was surrounded by little children dressed as angels with sparkling wings. Each group had a band which played gay marches rather than religious music. Other men walking with the band carried torches of twisted fibre dipped in pitch which gave off fragrance as well as light.

"The lanterns were the things of greatest beauty and most characteristic. An especially pretty type of lantern was of rose and cream colored paper. Other lanterns resembled full moons of creamy gold. Still others were shaped as stars; and last of all some pale green tulips came bobbing into the plaza to complete the rich bouquet.

"The final picture of the evening was seeing the devout marchers winding their way through the narrow streets back to their own *barrios*. We followed a line of pink tulips as they passed through the tree bordered entrance of a nearby church. The great door stood open to its full height to receive them while the music of the organ announced the beginning of the Mass."

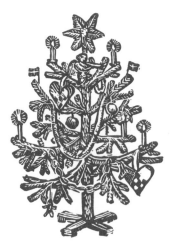

112

Peru

For several centuries Cusco, the ancient Inca capital of Peru, has contributed richly to the Christmas art of the world. In recent years, the work of the Quechua Indians has attracted the attention of collectors who marvel at the naïve charm of this pre-Columbian folk art. Of special interest are the *crèche* figures made in a variety of sizes for churches and private homes, particularly the Madonnas and the Wise Men which are cherished for their unique charm. Not only the techniques employed but also the facial expressions and the manner of modeling date back to the sixteenth century, when Pizarro claimed this land for Spain. Plaster, fabrics of various kinds, crude clay, and wood are the raw materials these primitive craftsmen use to make the figures currently sold in shops in various parts of the United States.

On rare occasions, one sees an heirloom Madonna and Child of the Cusco school painted on canvas. A far cry, indeed, from the humble attire usually associated with Mary is the regal portrayal of the Virgin clothed in rich robes and wearing a hat with plumage. The Christ Child has the appearance of a member of the Spanish royal family of the sixteenth century and appears in elaborate raiment as a rather grown-up child.

In Lima, Christmas is both a church holiday and the occasion for the great bullfight of the year. At its conclusion, an elaborate procession is held in which a statue of the Virgin figures conspicuously.

An unusual ceremony known as the Dance of the Beasts and Birds is part of the Christmas observance in the Huancayo district of Peru. Masked figures wearing spectacular headdresses of feathers parade through the church square led by black-faced miners. As they make their way down from the nearby mountains, the performers use rope made of llama wool to snare animals in the nearby woods. Those best suited are used in the manger settings within the church.

Puerto Rico

Early in the Christmas season, small bands of carolers, known as *trullas* or *parrandas,* make the rounds in Puerto Rico singing the traditional songs of the season. Often these visits are made as a surprise to serenade friends and neighbors and they always end with a feast of good things to eat and drink—in fact, it is not at all unusual for a family to go into debt in order to provide a bounteous table for the performers since the custom is an integral part of Christmas. Gifts of money are sometimes given to the *trullas* who often travel on horseback in rural areas. As they move from *finca* to *finca* (farm to farm), their numbers increase so that by early morning one may find the population of a whole mountainside singing happily under the roof of one small but hospitable home.

The songs they sing are known as *aguinaldos* and *villancicos,* Spanish Christmas carols with themes built around the Nativity with special emphasis on the

113

Three Kings and the gifts which they bring to the Christ Child. Among the instruments used by these roaming carolers are the *cuatro* (a four-stringed guitar), the *güiro* or *güícharo* (a long serrated gourd, scraped with a metal strip), and the six-stringed Spanish guitar. *Maracas,* made of dried round gourds with pebbles or dried seeds inside, and resonant sticks are popular modern-day additions to these rustic orchestras. The music of the *aguinaldo* is light and joyous, and while it is never an accompaniment for dancing, it is nevertheless popular in social gatherings where dance music is being played.

In the days when neighborhood *parrandas* or *trullas* were more commonplace, it was the tradition to hold open house for the musicians and the singers and serve such Christmas dishes as *arroz con dulce* (a kind of rice pudding), *longanizas, butifarras* and *morcillas* (three kinds of sausages), *pasteles* and *lechón asado* (barbecued pig). This custom has not disappeared by any means, but today the *trullas* come from greater distances and are not always known to those whom they serenade. They often wear fantastic costumes suggested by the Oriental dress of the Magi.

Santos, small hand-carved religious figures (Puerto Rico's oldest expression of art, dating back to the sixteenth century), are prominently displayed in homes at Christmas. The earliest *santos* were carved from a single piece of native wood, such as *mastic* and *caoba* (mahogany). Later, imported woods like pine, fir, and oak were used, and the *santero* began to carve his figures in sections, either gluing them together or fastening the parts of the figures with wooden pegs. The statuettes are usually images of saints, including the familiar Nativity figures and the Three Kings, special favorites.

Each year at Christmas, crowds of children in Puerto Rico make a pilgrimage to the Church of San José at La Navidad on the offshore island of Hispaniola to see the animated *nacimiento*. This historic church contains a crucifix and an altar that date back to the year 1523—presented by Ponce de Leon and his daughter Leonor during the time they worshiped there. This particular *nacimiento* is one of the mechanical wonders of Central America. In many ways it resembles a mechanized toy village with all the inhabitants busily engaged in their various occupations, or traveling on tiny trains which run through the tiny village. In some ways it suggests the *putz,* or Christmas yard, popular with the Pennsylvania Dutch.

Beginning nine days before Christmas, the islanders in Puerto Rico attend the Mass of the Carols each day at five-thirty in the morning, and they continue to sing carols as they walk back to their homes or to work. Christmas Eve is a time of rejoicing, feasting, and entertaining. At midnight the people attend the Mass of the Rooster. As mentioned before, Spanish legend has it that the only time the rooster ever crowed at midnight was to announce the birth of the Infant Jesus. At the conclusion of the high Mass, the vested priest approaches the manger in the church and carries the statue of the Infant to the altar rail so that all may adore him.

Santa Claus and the Christmas tree have invaded Puerto Rico in recent years. In fact, North American customs have been introduced extensively because of the large number of Puerto Ricans who live in the major cities of the United States. Yet, the religious significance of the day and the season has not been

relegated to the background as much as one might expect. The introduction of Santa Claus and the Christmas tree are most welcome innovations for the children since they thus have two very special occasions, Christmas and Epiphany, only twelve days apart, when they can look forward to receiving gifts. The fact that such demands may be a bit strenuous for parents is seldom mentioned.

Children have a special fondness for the Feast of Epiphany. In recent years, the old tradition of gift-giving at this time has been revived in a very special way by Doña Felisa Rincon de Gautier, perennial mayoress of San Juan. On the eve of Three Kings Day, the children place water, a box of grass, and perhaps some grain under their beds for the weary horses or camels to enjoy. Gifts are left in place of the greens and each child has his favorite among the Wise Men. Not one but three days comprise the elaborate reception given to the Magi, extending Epiphany to January 8th.

On January 12th, known as Bethlehem Day, the children parade in still further tribute to the Magi. On this day, in various communities, three youngsters especially selected for the occasion ride astride ponies bearing gifts for the Christ Child as they parade through the center of town. They are followed by angels, shepherds, and musicians in colorful dress. Christmas is, indeed, a long, pleasant season in Puerto Rico, beginning on December 16th and ending on January 12th.

Venezuela

The Venezuelan capital of Caracas celebrates Christmas Eve with a custom particularly popular with the teen-agers. Shortly after midnight, the handsome *prado*, Avenida de los Caiboas, fills with hundreds of young roller-skaters. Schoolmates and friends form congenial groups and skate together for an hour or two, until time for the special Mass that is always held for them. At the church door they are welcomed with gay music, folk tunes, and *villancicos* played on the harp as well as on the guitar, the *maracas*, and the barrel-shaped *furnco*. After the service, the young people skate home, arriving ravenously hungry for the breakfast of hearty *hallacas*, without which Christmas in Venezuela would not seem like Christmas.

The traditional national dish served at Christmas—*hallacas* (pronounced ah-yácas) is, in fact, a way of life in Venezuela, frequently requiring two days to a week to prepare, with the whole family participating. An *hallaca* is a meat pie with a cornmeal crust, flavored with herbs, condiments, and wine, wrapped in banana leaves and boiled in water. It is served on saints' days, at christenings, and during the Christmas season. A platter of *hallacas* calls for a family's finest linens, china, and silverware. Although it has never been quite determined whether *hallacas* are of Spanish or Indian origin, or a combination of both, they are not to be found anywhere else in the world, and each household uses its own recipe with great family pride.

Located in the western part of the country, fifty-three hundred feet above sea level, is the historic city of Mérida, made famous by Bolivar when he was hailed

115

as the Great Liberator in 1813. Residents of this old university city cling to many colorful legends, among which is a curious Christmas custom known as *La Paradura del Niño*—the Standing Up of the Christ Child. In 1958, when the city celebrated its four hundredth anniversary, this quaint local fiesta was considered important enough to be included in *IV Centenario,* Mérida's official history.

Katharine Van Etten Lyford, noted collector of the folklore and traditions of Latin America, has given us a lively account of it: "Merideños begin preparations for Christmas about the middle of December. Every family, rich or poor, builds a *pesebre* or manger scene which becomes the center of family life until February when it is dismantled. Some *pesebres* are small enough to be placed on a table but frequently others are so large that they fill an entire room. Chairs and tables covered with paper or cloth are converted into mountains or plains, moss is used for pastures and cotton creates the illusion of rushing rivers and waterfalls. Occasionally families try to reproduce the historic background of Bethlehem, but a local setting is more usual. This features Mérida's three rivers at the base of broad mountain slopes cut into curious shapes by high *apartaderos* (stone walls). The steep upper levels beyond the tree line are brightened with bunches of the yellow furry-leaved *frailejones*—the eidelweiss of the Andes. And above them the five "white eagles" of the Andes, named Bolivar, Humboldt, Bonplan, Lión and Bull.

"Figures are carved out of *aníme* (a delicate balsa wood from nearby forests) to represent farmers, hunters, soccer players, secretaries (at their typewriters), students and housewives—and folks busy at all kinds of local industries. To these are added pottery or wooden angels, shepherds, sheep, dogs, cats, palm-thatched *casitas* (huts) and chapels. Modern touches are provided by bulldozers, a policeman on a motor bike, a model of the Mérida-Caracas airplane or a miniature of the *telesférico* (cable car) that carries passengers seven miles straight up from tropical Mérida to the snow fields in less than an hour—the highest cable car in the world.

"By the day before Christmas, the *pesebre* is ready for the finishing touches of flowers and lights. Then the Holy Family is placed in the center of the scene with the adoring angels and animals nearby and the Wise Men far enough away so that they may be moved closer to the Christ Child each day, thus reenacting their traditional journey to Bethlehem.

"Visiting manger scenes is a popular entertainment during the holidays and prizes are offered for those judged the most unusual or most beautiful. In many homes it is traditional for the family to say the Rosary or evening prayers in front of the *pesebre*. But it is not until New Year's Day that the Paradura Del Niño takes place.

"In Mérida, custom decrees that on the first day of the New Year the figure of the Christ Child must be lifted from the crib and placed in a standing position—and remain standing until the Feast of Candelaria on February 2. Neighbors and friends keep watch to be sure the tradition is strictly honored—at the same time hoping someone will forget and thereby pay the forfeit of a Paradura party. When the grapevine telegraph reports that a figure of the Holy Child is still lying in the crib, neighbors secretly arrange to steal the Babe and

116

hide it. The careless owner knows only too well that it is useless to hunt—the only way he can recover his stolen Niño (Child) is to give a party to the kidnapping neighbors and friends.

"A Paradura party is no small affair. First of all, godparents must be chosen, two men and two women, so that each may hold a corner of the big silk handkerchief in which the Christ Child will be carried back to the *pesebre*. (If a basket is to be used instead, only two godparents are needed.)

"A Paradura godfather has many responsibilities. He must preside over the traditional procession and pay for the refreshments of the party that follows. Tall, ribbon-trimmed candles must be provided for the other godparents and smaller ones for all the marchers. His also is the privilege of paying for fireworks to be set off by a bevy of exuberant small boys forming an advance guard, and the *conjunto* (orchestra composed of guitar, maracas, violin and *cuatro*) that will play during the triumphant return of the Christ Child to his *pesebre*.

"As the Paradura usually takes place in the evening, the host and his family spend the day cleaning and dusting the house from which the Child has been stolen and borrowing chairs and dishes from obliging neighbors. The arrival of the godparents in front of the empty crib soon after dark is the signal for the procession to assemble. At a nod from the godfather, members line up in time-honored order. First come the boys, only too eager to lead the way through the dark streets, flourishing sparklers and exploding firecrackers to announce the beginning of the Paradura. Behind them walk the musicians, silent now, for they will not play until El Niño has been found.

"Teen-agers dressed as Mary and Joseph come next, preceded by a little señorita carrying a large star. Mary is usually riding a donkey with Joseph walking beside her. Follow the Magi, boys dressed in home-made attempts at oriental splendor, their new dignity marred now and then by the refractory conduct of the puzzled work mules on which they are mounted. Children in the costumes of shepherds precede the godparents carrying the empty handkerchief, singing the ancient Paradura carol:

> " 'Come we now to search for the Child
> Who has been stolen from this house.
> Come now, Shepherds, come now
> Come we altogether.'

"The song is picked up by other marchers and soon the streets are echoing with it. The colorful procession is a ribbon of candle light as it winds its way slowly toward the house where the stolen Christ Child is rumored to be hidden. When the godparents arrive at the door and ask for the Child, the little figure is promptly surrendered and placed in the middle of the handkerchief. At this moment the music begins, violin, guitar and the four-stringed *cuatro* blending with the maracas in a happy outburst of Christmas song. Now it is time for the shepherds to sing another carol, this time to announce—

> " 'Here we find the Child
> Who we thought was lost
> Now we'll take him to his home
> And his godparents shall carry him.'

"Endless verses of this familiar carol are sung by the Wise Men, by Saint Joseph and by the Virgin Mary as the recessional wends its triumphant way back to the house of the *pesebre* with the empty crib. There, standing before the manger, the godparents kiss the figure of the Babe of Bethlehem, then hold him out to the guests who press forward to pay their homage in the same way. Meanwhile the shepherds are singing again—

> " 'Godparents and shepherds,
> We come to kiss the Child,—
> This sacred kiss
> We give with affection.
> And as we give this kiss
> To the blessed Child Jesus
> The godparents will stand him up
> And he will remain standing.'

"Once the figure of the little Christ is placed erect, the youngest guests crowd forward to take their part in the Paradura. Hoisted on to chairs or tables, or held high in the arms of proud parents, these toddlers make their *ofrendas* (gifts) —plus rhymes or jingles they have been taught for this important occasion.

"A diminutive señorita of three thrusts a rumpled package at the *pesebre*. In timid babytalk, made no clearer by a dimpled finger in her mouth, she lisps—

> " 'I am a poor gypsy
> Who comes from Japan
> To offer the Child
> This tart made of ham.'

"As the guests shout with laughter, she buries her head in her mother's skirts. Then a sturdy muchacho, a year or two her senior, climbs down from his father's shoulder and walks bravely to the manger scene. Placing his gift at the feet of the Christ Child with obvious reluctance, he faces the guests—and forgets his rhyme. Prompted by his father he recites in a strident shout—

> " 'I am a little shepherd,
> Who comes from Bailadores
> And I bring the Child Jesus
> This pack of *voladores* (firecrackers).'

"More laughter when a third child, whose shepherd's costume drags on the floor, holds out a candle much the worse for being squeezed in a hot, grubby hand. His tired little smile reveals two missing front teeth whose absence has a curious effect on his Spanish consonants. He intones solemnly—

> " 'I am a little boy
> Who comes from Asulita
> To offer to the Child
> Just this small *velita* (candle).' "

The godfather of the Paradura sees that all the children have a chance to take part in the *Ofrenda,* then gives way to the women guests. They gather about the *pesebre* and together recite the rosary.

118

In the meantime, impatient guests have been hovering about the patio and the front door, eagerly waiting the godfather's invitation to share the wine and cookies he has provided as refreshment. At his order, the *conjunto* begins to play and soon the house is full of dancing guests. As happy couples whirl past him, he has only one more responsibility—aside from paying the bills. This is to be sure that, if there is any dancing in the room of the *pesebre,* the standing figure of the Babe of Bethlehem is carefully covered with a handkerchief *"para no faltarle el respeto"*—to ensure no lack of respect. With refreshments and dancing the hours pass swiftly until a pale light touches the five "white eagles" announcing the coming of dawn and therewith the end of the Paradura Del Niño.

China

Christmas has been known to some of the Chinese people for about four hundred years, but less than 1 per cent of the population of this vast country is Christian. Thus, to the great majority, Christmas and its meaning are beyond their realm of understanding. Chinese Christians call this feast day *Sheng Dan Jieh* (Holy Birth Festival) and the Christmas tree is appropriately called the Tree of Light. When we consider the cultural background of this ancient nation and its contribution to every phase of man's intellectual development, it is perhaps not too surprising to find precise language used to describe those things the Chinese hold sacred.

Children hang up stockings (made of muslin especially for the occasion) and expect *Lan Khoong-Khoong* (Nice Old Father) to fill them. In China, Santa Claus is also known as *Dun Che Lao Ren* (Christmas Old Man). Because of their love of brilliant color and glitter, the Chinese greatly enjoy our Western Christmas decorations and have made extensive use of their own colorful paper lanterns for holiday decorations. Those who exchange gifts adhere closely to their own tradition regarding presents. Choice and costly presents are given only to members of the family, while those of remembrance value are for friends and distant relatives. Fireworks such as are used in southern Europe, in Latin America, and in the South in our country have their place in China to usher in Christmas. It is a time of feasting and merrymaking, with jugglers and acrobats contributing their talents to this new festival adopted from the Christian world.

In their delightful book, *A New Look at Christmas Decorations,* Sister M. Gratia Listaite and Norbert A. Hildebrand have created many original decorations based on old Chinese symbols which are suggested as appropriate for a tree typical of the feeling and sentiment of China. A "ricksha model, fashioned of paper and pipe cleaners, makes an unusual tree ornament, or it may be used for a table centerpiece. Butterflies and moths, which appear in many

120

forms of Chinese art, are well suited for those who like their ornaments intricate and artistic. Simpler, but equally effective, are the paper silhouettes of ancient Chinese temples, and mobiles made to resemble Chinese kites. The traditional lanterns make shades to give even American Christmas tree lights an oriental appearance."

Decorations made of colored paper and evergreens are used in the Christian homes and churches in China. Brightly hued paper chains, posters carrying messages of peace and joy, and paper flowers for the tree are typical of the ornaments. Paper lanterns are used in the church services at Christmas.

The Chinese New Year, which begins in late January or early February, depending on the position of the moon, is a week-long celebration: the most important of the year. On the last day of the old year, accounts are settled by business men in every type of enterprise. It is also a day of feasting, ceremony, and firecrackers. Gilt paper is burned on a charcoal brazier both before and after the dinner, which is served to the head of the house by the younger sons. Then the remains of the smoldering gilt paper are divided into twelve piles—one for each month. The time required for the flame of each pile to die out indicates the changes from rain to drought that can be expected during the year.

The first celebration on New Year's Day is the offering made to heaven and earth. Rice, vegetables, tea, wine, candles, and incense are used in the ceremony. Tribute is paid to ancestors and to all living members of the family. Chinese homes are elaborately decorated for this festival with brightly colored banners (unless the family is in mourning), bearing expressions of happiness and expressing ambitions for the coming year. Business is suspended during this time of rejoicing, and in the past considerable sums of money were spent on fireworks. Gifts are exchanged, new clothes are worn, and the children have their share of toys and fireworks, too. The Feast of the Lanterns is the great spectacle of the week and no one is so poor that he does not have at least one lantern to light for the occasion. This is also the time for the Festival of the Dragons and the Fisherman's Festival. Every nation has its own collection of unusual folk beliefs. In China it is considered unlucky to meet a woman when you leave home, for the first time, on New Year's Day.

Japan

In Japan, where numerous festivals are held throughout the year, lanterns and flowers, children and ancestors, flags and dolls and the various seasons as well come in for their share of tribute. Pageantry and ceremonial are as much a part of life as the gracious manners and the high standard of decorum which are so characteristically Japanese. The birthday of the Christ Child is comparatively new to them, dating back only about a hundred years. Even today, as in China, the Christian population is less than 1 per cent, and a similar situation exists in Korea and on the Island of Formosa.

121

Actually, Christmas was little known in Japan until the beginning of this century, but it has become widely familiar, particularly in the last two decades, because of the millions of decorations and trinkets and the ever-growing number of products manufactured in Japan for the Christmas markets of the world (notably those of the United States). While missionaries of many creeds paved the way, radio, television, newspapers and magazines, the exchange of foreign students, and commercial enterprise have all contributed immeasurably to the popularization of Christmas among those who do not profess Christianity. Visitors to the leading cities of Japan during the holiday season describe the preparations for Christmas as being so similar to those that we know in America and Europe that even the special Christmas sales have a familiar ring. The hustle and bustle of Christmas shopping, the fancy ornaments and gadgets and all the fanfare of the Western World have reached Japan, creating a business boom of surprising proportions.

Each year, in increasing numbers, the Japanese exchange gifts, eat turkey for Christmas dinner, and, in some communities, even have community Christmas trees. The decorative uses of mistletoe and holly are familiar to many of them, as are our carols, which they sing in their own language. *Hoteiosho,* one of their gods, serves as Santa Claus for their children. Elizabeth Hough Sechrist tells us in *Christmas Everywhere* that this kind old man is supposed to have eyes in the back of his head so that he can observe children's behavior.

However, New Year's Day, *Oshogatsu,* is the leading holiday in Japan. This is the time when houses are given a thorough cleaning before they are decorated. Branches of pine are attached to the entrance gates of the homes, and both pine and bamboo have a place of special importance at the family shrine indoors as symbols of long life. Ropes of twisted rice straw, hung above the gates, mean strong family ties, and, when the tiny Japanese oranges are added, they signify "roundness and smoothness." Families dress in their best clothes to pay visits to their friends, and they never fail to pay tribute to their ancestors and departed members of the family on this day. Ceremonies are held at home to drive out the evil spirits. Dried beans tossed into the corner of every room are the means by which evil is dispelled, to be replaced with good fortune.

Japanese children make the most of the occasion, with the boys flying kites and the girls enjoying favorite games. The boys also organize small bands composed of drums, cymbals, and the flute, and go about playing for the amusement of their elders and all who care to listen. This performance is in mimicry of adults who go about as maskers, performing in a similar manner. Toys are used at New Year's to decorate the branches of trees and are carried about for the amusement of the children, who later receive them as gifts. In many ways, the Japanese New Year celebration resembles Christmas in the Western World. Business establishments are closed for three days and it is truly a family festival in which devotion to the home is uppermost.

Australia

Australia, among the newest nations of the world, was settled predominantly by natives of the British Isles. Their heritage of Christmas—the folklore they knew and loved and the customs they had enjoyed—were deeply rooted. What could they do to nurture them in the new country? The climate was vastly different, being both hot and dry. The rich, heavy food and the fireside socials which had made Christmas at home so memorable seemed not to fit in with the summer weather of the Australian holiday season. To be sure, Christmas everywhere is a time to reminisce, to talk of home and family and how the holidays were spent in earlier years, and this pastime the new settlers could enjoy. But, regardless of the fact that Christmas came at midsummer, the nostalgic carols they were used to singing lived on. Some were written down while others were kept alive in the memories of those who loved them. The familiar words, the haunting melodies, the lively tunes—all spelled out the Christmas they longed for, its sentiment and its traditions.

In *The Story of Christmas,* Michael Harrison tells how a new custom was developed from this deeply rooted Old World tradition, brought thousands of miles across the sea. On Christmas Eve in 1937, an Australian radio announcer, Norman Banks, was sitting in his flat gazing out the window. He heard a carol issuing from the radio of a nearby house and, looking out, saw an old lady listening "with an expression of rapt attention on her face. She held a candle in her hand as she listened—and it was this fact which caught Banks' attention, caught it, held it, and set his imagination leaping ahead of time and place. 'Carols by candlelight!' he whispered—and, in that moment, perhaps the most modern of all traditions was born."

Christmas is a rare time of year. It stirs men's hearts. Norman Banks was deeply moved by another incident—the memory of a child whom he had seen that very day in a Melbourne hospital, a victim of infantile paralysis. On the one hand, the old lady, when she heard the carol, became nostalgic of heart, while

123

the crippled child was living in a realm of darkness. The two thoughts began to fuse in Banks' mind. What could be done to lift hearts like these? By the following Christmas Eve, he had arranged for carol singing in Alexandra Gardens, along the river in Melbourne. Thus, was launched "Carols by Candlelight," an annual event in which thousands of all ages and creeds take part every year. It is broadcast and sent all over the world. On Christmas Eve in 1943, the "Melbourne Carol" with words and music by Norman Banks was sung for the first time in Alexandra Gardens.

> Yuletide in Melbourne means mass jubilation
> And carols by candlelight on Christmas Eve
> Thousands assemble in glad dedication
> To hail him with joy, and the vow—"I believe."

As Michael Harrison has stated, "There have been better carols, but never an earlier Antipodean one. It deserves social recognition for this fact alone. Honour to the Pioneer!" The "Melbourne Carol" has been recorded by St. Patrick's Cathedral Choir in New York City and sold for the benefit both of children afflicted with infantile paralysis and of blind babies.

Depending on where you live in Australia, it is Father Christmas or Santa Claus who brings the gifts. While dinner may be traditional on Christmas Day, supper is likely to be a picnic at the beach or in the country. Ferns, flowers, and foliage, including the Christmas Bell and the Christmas Bush, are used for decoration during the holiday season. The day after Christmas is usually a pleasant one for a picnic.

Index

Abrams, Freda Morrill, 82
Abyssinians, 18
Adam and Eve, 48
Advent, 30, 53, 54, 68, 73
Advent wreath, 53, 100
Agassiz, Louis, 100
Aguinaldos, 97, 114
Air plants, 111
Aix, 46
Aladdin, 40
Alameda, 111
Albert, Prince, 38
Alexandra Gardens, 124
Almond, magic, 32
Almond soap, 78
Alps, 64
Alsace, 44, 45, 51
America, 23, 77
Amsterdam, 60
Andersen, Hans C., 31, 90

Andes, 102, 116
Animals, 26, 30, 32, 48, 70, 72, 73, 77, 88, 105
Aníme, 116
Anthesteria Festival, 56
Antioquía, 102
Apennines, 64
Apple, 30, 48, 51, 53, 87, 92, 105
Applesticks, 87
April Fool's Day, 99
Arabian Nights, 67
Arepas, 102
Aristotle, 36
Armenian Church, 18
Arroz con dulce, 114
Ash tree, 37
Ashen faggot, 33, 37
Asia Minor, 57
Ass, the, 64
Atlanta, Ga., 21
Aubagne, 46
Auld Lang Syne, 77

Auriol, 46
Australia, 77, 123, 124
Austria, 25, 26, 27, 37
Avenida de los Caiboas, 115
Azuela de ave, 102

Babouschka, 69, 74
Bagpipes, 69
Baking Day, 32
Balsa wood, 116
Balthazar, 83
Bambuco, 96, 102
Banks, Norman, 123
Bannocks, 77
Barcelona, 79
Bari, 57
Barley, 72
"Barn elf," 70
Barring the Schoolmaster, 98
"Barrios," 112
Bartoumieu, 46

Basil, 55
Basilica, the Great, 18
Batidos, 106
Baton Rouge, La., 21
Baubles, 49, 53
Baudouin, 42
Bavaria, 42, 47
Bay, 36
Beacon Hill, 21
Beatrix, Princess, 61
Befana, 69, 74
Belgium, 27, 84
Bells, 14, 44, 77, 90, 92, 124
  ringing of, 32, 36, 37
Berlinerkranser, 72
"Bernie Bough," 33
Bethlehem, 14, 18, 23, 35, 46, 64, 65, 69, 73, 74, 83, 92, 97, 103, 104, 107, 108, 110, 116, 117
  Star of, 63, 73, 92

Bethlehem Day, 115
Bethlehem 1933, 45
"Bethlehems," 29
Bishop money, 59
Black Man, 59
Black Peter, 57, 59, 60, 61
Blessing the water, 56, 75
Blycido, 75
Boar's head, 33, 36
Bocinas, 104, 105
Bohemia, 28, 30
Bolivar, 115
Bologna, Italy, 68
Bom Natal, 96
Bonaventure, St., 64
Bonfires, 56, 83
Boniface, St., 49
Boston, Mass., 21
Boxing Day, 40, 63
Bradford, Governor, 19
Brazil, 96, 100
"Bread of Angels," 75
Bretons, 44
British Isles, 33, 63, 96, 123
Broadway, England, 37
Bromeliads, 97
Brooks, Phillips, 17, 18
Brothers Grimm, 90
Brueghel, 28
Brunekager, 32
Bullfights, 96
Bunuelos, 102, 106
Burgundy, 44
"Burial of the Gold," 76
"Buskers," 40
Butler, Harriet, 24

Cacastes, 106
Caesar, 51
Cake Day, 72
"Cake-of-the-year," 63
Calta, 30
Candelaria, Feast of, 116
Candles, 30, 32, 59, 62, 72, 73, 84, 85, 87, 92, 97, 100, 101, 102, 106, 107, 108, 117, 119, 121, 123
Canute, King, 90
Caoba, 114
Capitone, 68
Capri, 65
Caracas, 115
Carillons, 44
Carinthia, 25
Carlo III, King, 65

"Carol of the Birds," 81
Carol-singers, 33, 40
Carols, 14, 21, 26, 37, 40, 44, 62, 63, 68, 73, 74, 82, 95, 97, 104, 114, 117, 122, 123
meaning of, 40
"Carols by Candle-light," 124
Carp, 25, 30
Carrots, 83
Carthaginians, 78
Casals, Pablo, 81
Cat, 33
Catalan, 82
Catalonia, 81
Cattle, blessing of, 72
Celetna, 30
Cena, 97, 100, 107
Centenario IV, 116
Central America, 99
Cert, 29
Charlemagne, 42
Cherry blossoms, 30
Chestnuts, 44, 78
Children's Friend, The, 23
Chile, 101
Chimney, 56, 59, 76
China, 121
Chipping Campden, England, 37
Choirboys, 57
Christ Child, 14, 18, 26, 28, 32, 44, 46, 48, 49, 51, 54, 62, 64, 67, 73, 74, 75, 78, 79, 92, 97, 100, 101, 103, 104, 105, 107, 108, 110, 112, 113, 114, 115, 116, 117, 118, 121
Standing Up of the, 116
Christkind, The, 25
Christkindli, 92
Christmas and Its Customs, 72
Christmas Book, The, 26, 75, 79
"Christmas bread," 30, 31, 54, 102
"Christmas buck," 70
Christmas Bush, 124
Christmas cake, 38, 44, 55, 68
Christmas cards, 21
Christmas cookies, 59, 84, 85, 90, 92, 105, 111
Christmas cribs, 46, 47, 51, 53, 65, 67, 97, 107

Christmas Customs Around the World, 28
Christmas decorations, 48
Christmas Eve, 36, 48, 49, 54, 55, 56, 61, 62, 63, 64, 68, 70, 73, 74, 75, 84, 87, 88, 92, 94, 96, 97, 100, 103, 110, 111, 112, 114, 115, 123
Christmas Everywhere, 122
Christmas Fantasy, A, 111
Christmas fire, 32
Christmas on the Hacienda, 104
Christmas loaf, 54, 55
Christmas log, 56
Christmas market, 53
Christmas Old Man, 120
"Christmas pig," 54, 56, 70, 96, 102, 114
Christmas plates, 31
Christmas plays, 45
Christmas in Ritual and Tradition, 25
Christmas rose, 108
Christmas seal, 31
Christmas tree, 21, 23, 27, 29, 32, 37, 38, 42, 48, 49, 51, 53, 61, 62, 70, 72, 74, 79, 87, 88, 92, 99, 103, 107, 114, 115, 120
Community, 21, 45
Christmas Yards, 23, 114
Christmas, meaning of, 13
"old fashioned," 33
old style, 18
Christmas, the Story of, 123
Christopsomo, 54
Chronia polla, 54
Church of the Nativity, 18
Church of San José, 114
Cinderella, 40
Civil War, 21
Cleansing of the Temple, 14
Cleveland, Ohio, 21
Clovis, 42
Coffee berries, 104
Colatzia, 75

Collo, 101
Colombia, 97, 99, 102
Columbus, 19
Constantinople, 74
Corn, sheaves of, 75
Coronitas, 104
Corpus Christi, 80
Costa Rica, 96, 97, 99, 102
Cotswold Country, 37
Coupling of fire, 56
Covenant, Ark of the, 79
Cracow, 73
Cradle-rocking, 51
Crèches, 42, 45, 47, 111, 113
Cromwell, Oliver, 63
Cross, 30, 54
Crowing of the Cock, 95
Cuatro, 114, 117
Cuba, 30
Cueca, 96
Cusco, 113
Cypress, 104
Czechoslovakia, 28, 29

da Todi, Jacopone, 67
"Daft days," 77
Daiken, Leslie, 35
Dallas, Tex., 21
Dance of the Beasts and Birds, 113
"Dance of the Six," 79
Dances, 80, 96, 100, 105
de Bouillon, Godefroy, 42
Decorations, 120
de Gallo, Missa, 97
de Gautier, Doña Felisa Rincon, 115
de Leon, Ponce, 114
de Robeck, Nesta, 64, 67
del Niño, 103
del Rosario, Virgin, 101
Demons, 56
Denmark, 31
Denver, Colo., 21
Devil, the, 59
Devil's Funeral, The, 63
Devil's Knell, Tolling the, 33, 36
Dewsbury, England, 36, 37
Dickens, Charles, 14, 21, 31, 33, 36, 42, 99
Diocletian, Emperor, 85

Dolls, 35, 45, 72, 104, 110, 122
Donkey, 83
Doppa i Grytan, 87
Dulcimer, 105
Dun Che Lao Ren, 120
Dunster, England, 37
Dutch Parliament, 61
Duyckinck, Jan, 23

Easter, 54, 80
Ecuador, 104
Edman, Gunnar, 84
Eggs, 105, 106
Eggshells, decorated, 45
Egypt, Flight into, 45
Eidelweiss, 116
Eisteddfoddes, 95
El Día de Guadalupe, 106
El Salvador, 97
"Elf's Porridge," 70
Elizabeth, Daughter of King James I, 28
Elizabeth, Queen, 40
Elves, 32, 76
England, 33, 36, 72, 77, 95
English Christmas, 21
Epiphany, 18, 25, 36, 54, 56, 69, 99, 100, 115
Epiphany Eve, 76, 83
Epiphytes, 111
Evergreens, 13, 61
Ex-votos, 53
Eynsham, England, 37

Fall of Man, 48
Farandole, 42
Farolitos, 106
Father Christmas, 59, 74, 94, 124
Feast of feasts, 64
Feast of the Lanterns, 121
Feast of the Nativity, 19
Feast of the Three Kings, 96
Ferias, 79
Festival of the Dragon, 121
Fir tree, 49
"Fir Tree, The," 31
Firecrackers, 97, 100, 104, 107, 117, 118, 121
Fireworks, 96, 101, 108, 117, 120, 121
First Christmas, 29
First Christmas Tree, The, 49

"First footing," 77, 78
Fisherman's Festival, 121
Flanders, 28
"Flower of Christmas Eve," 108
Foie Gras, 44
Football, 95
Formosa, Island of, 121
Fougasse cake, 46
Frailejones, 116
France, 42, 47, 63, 92, 99
Francis, St., 25, 40, 47, 64, 65, 67
Frankincense, 105
Freia, 70
Freyr, 36
Fruit trees, 30, 42, 55, 83
Furnco, 115
Furze, 62

Garden of Eden, 48
Garlands, 37, 85
Gaspar, 83
"Generous Eve," 29
Germany, 30, 38, 47, 48, 51, 90, 92, 107
Ginger, 106
Gingerbread, 27, 29
Giovanni, 64
Globo, 102, 103
Gloucester St., Duke of, 21
Gnome, 31, 33, 88
Goblin, 55
Goigs, 82
Gold, 105
"Good King Wenceslaus," 29
Goose, 25, 32, 44
Gourds, 106
Gourmet, 67
Grain, 76
Grandfather Frost, 74
Great Britain, 76, 99
Greccio, 64
Greece, 42, 55, 56, 74
Greek Calendar Customs, 55
Greek Orthodox Church, 13, 18 57
Gregorian Calendar, 18, 85
Gregory II, Pope, 49
Gruber, Franz, 26
Guatemala City, 106
Guitar, 117
Gundhar, 49
Gypsies, 28, 37, 46

Haakon, King, 70
Haiti, 96, 99

Hallacas, 115
Halliday, W. R., 92
Halloween, 98
Hampshire, 37
Harrison, Michael, 29, 123, 124
Hautboy, 40
Headcheese, 84
Herod, King, 45
Hertha, 51
Hilary, St., 84
Hildebrand, Norbert A., 120
Hirtenlieder, 25
Hispaniola, Island of, 114
Hjortetakk, 72
Hjul, 84
Hogmanay, 76, 77
Holboll, Einar, 31
Hole, Christina, 77
Holland, 57, 59, 60, 61, 62, 84, 99
Holly, 36, 37, 38, 53, 61, 62, 122
Holy Birth Festival, 120
Holy Communion, 73
Holy Family, 37, 45, 46, 62, 78, 97, 100, 104, 116
Holy Innocents' Day, 83, 96, 99
Holy Land, 18, 65
Holy Night, The, 13, 32
Holy water, 56
Honey, 54, 75, 82, 106
Horse races, 96
Hoteiosho, 122
House of Santa Claus Society, 24
Huancayo, 113
Hyanuary, 100

Icons, 53, 55
Ile-de-France, 44
Immaculate Conception, Feast of the, 79, 80, 96
Inca, 113
Incense, 30, 56
Indians, 104, 105, 106, 108, 111, 113, 115
Ireland, 62, 63
Irene, Princess, 61
Irving, Washington, 23, 31, 33, 36
Isabeau, Queen of Bavaria, 42
Ischia, 65
Italy, 25, 47, 57, 64, 67, 68, 69, 92, 99
Ivy, 37

Jack and the Bean Stalk, 40
Jack-in-the-box, 36
Jacopone, 25
Jaffa Gate, 18
James I, King, 29
Japan, 80, 121, 122
Jaquet-Droz, Pierre, 90
Jean-le-Bon, King, 42
Jicaras, 106
John XXII, Pope, 47
Joropo, 96
Joselki, 73
Joseph, 26, 62, 106, 107, 108, 110, 117, 118
Jourdan, 46, 47
Joyeuse Noël, 96
Judaism, 14
Judas, 90
Judea, 18
Julafton, 87
Julbrock, 84
Julebaal, 32
Julekake, 72
Julesvenn, 72
Julian Calendar, 18, 85
Juliana, Queen, 60, 61
Jultomten, 88

Kalanda, 54
Kalendae, 75
Kalends, 13, 14
Kallikantzaroi, 55, 56, 76
Kersmis, 13
Kios, 55
Kiosks, 97
Kissing Bunch, 37
Kissing Bunch Still Hangs High, The, 37
Kites, 120
Knickerbocker History, 23
Kollyva, 53
Kolya, 75
Kolyáda, 75
Kolyádki, 74
Korea, 121
Koutia, 75
Kozani, 54
Krampus, 25
Kris Kringle, 88

La Navidad, 114, 119
Lady Poverty, Feast of, 64
Lamb, offering of, 45
Lamp-lighters, 33
Lan Khoong-Khoong, 120
Lanterns, 121
Lapps, 74
Las Posadas, 108, 110

126

Latin America, 96, 116, 120
Laverty, Maura, 63
Le père Noël, 44
Le Réveillon, 44
Leo III, Pope, 42
León, 116
Leonor, 114
Les Baux, 45
Libanius, 14
Lima, 113
Listaite, Sister M. Gratia, 120
Litany of Loretto, 108
Lithuania, 45
Lititz, 23
Llamas, 97, 104, 105, 113
London, 35, 85
Longfellow, Henry Wadsworth, 69
"Lord God's Corner, The," 26
Lord of Misrule, 98
Los Pastores, 108
Los Seises, 79, 80
Lowther Arcade, 35
Lucia Day, 85
Lucia, St., 84, 85
"Lucky bird," 77
Luminarios, 108
Lutfisk, 87
Luther, Martin, 49, 51
Lyford, Katharine Van Etten, 38, 102, 104, 116
Lyons, 45

Macedonia, 54
Madonna, 69, 113
Maggiore, Lake, 63
Magi, 28, 65, 69, 82, 99, 115, 117
Mai, 45
Manaos, 101
Manger, 21, 45, 62, 64, 65, 68, 78, 92, 103, 104, 105, 113, 116
Maracas, 97, 102, 114, 115, 117
Margarido, 46
Marguerite, Queen of Navarre, 45
Mari Llwyd, 95
Marie, Saint of Bethlehem, 42
Marijke, Princess, 60
Marimba, 97, 106, 107
Marseilles, 46, 47
Mary, Virgin, 26, 44, 46, 54, 55, 62, 67, 101, 106, 107, 108, 110, 111, 113, 117, 118
Marzipan, 38

Marzipan pig, 32, 70
Masica, 30
Masquerade party, 30
Mass, of the Carols, 114
Midnight, 44, 45, 68, 78, 97, 100, 103, 104, 107, 112
of the Rooster, 97, 114
of the Shepherds, 74
Mastic, 114
Match-seller, 45
Maurel, Antoine, 46
Medellin, 102
Mediterranean, 82
Megas, George A., 55
Melbourne, 123
"Melbourne Carol," 123, 124
Melchior, 83
Mérida, 115
Meringue, 96
"Merry Christmas, Lovely Christmas," 32
Messenia, 54
Mexican flag, 108
Mexico, 97, 108, 111, 112
Middle Ages, 25, 45
Miles, Clement, 25, 75
Mince pies, 38
Minstrels, 69
Miracle Plays, 44, 45, 47, 48, 90
Missa de Gallo, 112
Mistletoe, 27, 33, 37, 122
Mithraic creed, 14
Mohammedans, 57
Mohr, Father Joseph, 26
Monte Rainerio, 64
Moore, Dr. Clement C., 23, 24
Moravian, 23
Mummers, 14, 23, 37, 78
Music boxes, 90
Myrrh, 105
Mystères de la Nativité, 45
Mystery plays, 44, 46, 47, 48

Nacimientos, 78, 79, 83, 96, 97, 107, 114
Nadolig, 95
Naples, 46, 65, 67, 69
Natale, 67
Nativity, 63, 65, 73, 75, 110, 114
Nativity plays, 28

Nazareth, 108
New Look at Christmas Decorations, A, 120
New Testament, 110
New Year, 68, 77, 78, 84
New Year Tree, 74
New Year's Day, 14, 23, 42, 45, 55, 63, 92, 95, 116, 121, 122
New Year's Eve, 27, 76, 107
New York, 21, 23, 85, 124
Newport, R. I., 24
Nice Old Father, 120
Nicholas of Pinora, 57
Nicholas, St., 23, 27, 29, 35, 51, 53, 54, 57, 59, 60, 61, 69, 72, 73, 74, 94
"Night Before Christmas, The," 24
"Night of Cakes," 63
Nisse, 31, 32, 33
Nobel, Alfred, 85
Nobel Prize, 85
Nochebuena, 78, 96
Noël, 13, 40, 44
North America, 33, 61, 76, 85, 111, 115
North Pole, 23
Norway, 70
Nougat, 68, 78
Nouvés, 44
Nuremberg, 53

"O Little Town of Bethlehem," 17
"O Tannenbaum," 28
Oak tree, 70
Oaxaca, 111, 112
Oberndorf, 26
Oboe, 40
Ofrenda, 118, 119
Old Bishop, 57
Old Testament, 110
Olive tree, 54
Ollas, 105
Onion, 94
Oplatki, 73
Orange, 36, 92, 105
Orchids, 102, 104, 111
Order of the Star, 42
Orient, 45
Ornaments, 92, 111
Orthodox Church, 74
Oshogatsu, 122
Oslo, Norway, 38
Our Lady of the Rosary, 82
Ox, the, 64
Oxford, England, 36

Oysters, 44

Pan Dolce, 68
Pan de pasqua, 102
Pan forte, 68
Pancake, 112
Panettone, 68
Pantomimes, 33, 40
Papa Noël, 99, 100, 101
Parade, 60, 85, 96, 106
Paradura, 118, 119
Paradura del Niño, 116
Paradura party, 117
Paramo, 97
Paris, 42, 44, 45, 85
Parrandas, 113, 114
Pasterka, 74
Pastorale, 46
Pastori, 65
Patrick, St., 62
Peaches, 101
Peep shows, 45, 47, 73
Pennsylvania, 23
Pennsylvania Dutch, 23, 114
Peru, 37, 113
Pesebre, 97, 100, 104, 116, 117, 118, 119
Peter, St., 49
Pharasa, 56
Philadelphia, Pa., 21, 23
Pifferari, 69
Pilgrims, 110
Piñatas, 108, 110
Pipes, Shepherds', 105
Pitching ye barr, 19
Pizarro, 113
Plum pudding, 38, 95
Plygain, 95
Plymouth Colony, 19
Podblyudnuiya, 75
Poems, 63, 92
Poinsettias, 21, 108
Poland, 30, 73
Politis, Nicholas, 56
Pontus, 54
"Poor man's cake," 72
Porridge, 70, 75, 88
Portals, 97, 103, 104
Portugal, 83, 99
Posadas, 97, 106, 107, 108
Prado, 115
Prague, 30
Presepio, 65, 67, 68
Pribram, 29
Provence, 28, 37, 42, 45, 46, 47, 83
Provence, Marcel, 47
Pudding, rice, 88
Puerto Rico, 97, 113, 114

Puestos, 108, 111
Punch and Judy, 40, 73
Puppet shows, 33, 45, 73
Puríssima, Feast of, 96, 97
Puritans, 76
Puss in Boots, 40
Putzes, 23, 114
Pyrenees, 80, 83

"Queen of Light," 85
Queen's College, Oxford, 36
Qüero, 114
Quícharo, 114

Rachel's Well, 18
Racines, 46
Radish Night, 111
Radishes, 111
Remi, Bishop, 42
Réveillon, 45
Rheims, 42
Rice, Charles D., 24
Riggs, Arthur Stanley, 80
Riis, Jacob, 31
Rio, 100
Rio Grande, 96
Riviera, 64
River Jordan, 18
Rocco, Maria Gregorio, 65
Romanche, 92
Rome, 13, 14, 49, 64, 68, 69, 79
Rondadores, 97
Roquevain, 46
Rosalia, St., 101
Rosary, 107, 108, 119
Rosemary, 36
Rosers, 82
Russia, 69, 74, 75

Sabbath, Hebrew, 79
Sabots, 44
Sacred Host, 48, 73
St. Gennaro, Order of, 65
St. John the Baptist, 27
St. Knut's Day, 90
St. Lucia, Feast of, 84
St. Nicholas Day, 84
St. Nicholas Eve, 61
St. Patrick's Cathedral Choir, 124
St. Stephen's Day, 31, 62, 63, 88
St. Sylvester's Eve, 74
Salzburg, 51
Samichlaus, 94
Samoyeds, 74
San Diego, Calif., 21
San Domingo, 19

San José, 97, 104
San Juan, 115
Santa Claus, 21, 23, 24, 57, 60, 72, 88, 92, 94, 99, 100, 101, 103, 114, 115, 120, 122, 124
Santa Maria, 19
Santi Belli, 46
Santiago, 106
Santíssimo Sacramento, 80
Santons, 28, 45, 46, 47
Santos, 114
São Paulo, 100
Sardana, 82
Saturn, 13
Saturnalia, 13
Sawdust, 97, 104
Scandinavia, 31, 70, 96
Scotland, 76, 78
Seattle, Wash., 21
Sechrist, Elizabeth Hough, 122
Second Christmas, 29, 62
Seville, 79, 80
Shattuck, Virginia C., 111
Sheng Dan Jieh, 120
Shepherd, 45, 65, 97
Shepherds' Field, 18
Shoes, 30, 44, 59
Shortbread, 77
Shotover, 36
Shrines, 67, 69
Shrovetide, 30
Sicily, 68, 69, 85
"Silent Night! Holy Night!," 26
Sinterklaas, 57, 59, 60, 61
"Sixes, The," 80
Skansen, 87
Skarkantzalos, 56
Slavic countries, 96
"Smoke Blessing," 26
Solstice, winter, 13
South America, 99, 111
Spain, 78, 79, 80, 83, 97, 99, 110, 113
Spanish Pageant, The, 80
"Speed the Plough," 33
Speculaas, 59
Spruce, 38
Star, 30, 87, 90, 117
Star Boys, 73, 90
Star Man, 73
Steen, Jan, 59
"Stephening," 31
Stockholm, 85, 87

Stockings, hanging of, 35, 120
Stoole-ball, 19
Stortorget Square, 87
Story of Christmas, The, 29
Strasbourg, 51
Straw, 72, 74, 75, 83, 84, 87, 122
Street, James, 36
"Surprises," 61
Svaty Mikalas Day, 29
Sweden, 63, 84, 85, 87, 88
Switzerland, 90, 92, 94
Sylte, 70
Sylvester, 27
Syrians, 18

Taai-taai, 59
Tamales, 104
Tehauna, 111
Tell, William, 90
Teutons, 14
Thanksgiving, 61
Theaters, traveling, 73
Thomas, St., 27
Thor, 36, 49, 51, 70, 84
Thrace, 54, 55
Three Kings, 100, 110, 114
Three Kings Day, 115
Tinsel, 53, 87
Tjugondag Knut, 84
Torches, 112
Tortellini, 68
Tortillas, 106
Toy makers, 53
Toyland, 51
Toy peddlers, 33, 35
Toys, 35, 38, 42, 47, 90, 97, 104, 108, 111, 114
    mechanical, 90
Toys Through the Ages, 23
Trafalgar Square, 38, 70
Trapp family, 26
"Trate," 63
Tree of Light, 120
Tree, world, 55
Triggel, 90
Trinity Church, 17
Troy, N. Y., 24
Troy Sentinel, The, 24
Trullas, 97, 113, 114
Tulips, 112
Turkey, 40, 44, 78, 122
Turrón, 78
Twelfth Night, 53, 63, 90

"Twelve Nights, The," 14
Tyrol, 26, 47

Unconquered Sun, 14
United States, 19, 92, 99, 103, 104, 107, 110, 113, 115, 122
Urn of Fate, 42, 79

Van Alen, James, 24
Van Dyke, Henry, 49
Van Nierop, Henriette, 57
Vellita, Giovanni, 64
Venezuela, 115
Victoria, Queen, 38
Viejo Pascuero, 101
Vikings, 36
Villancicos, 97, 114, 115
"Visit from St. Nicholas, A," 23
Vladimir the Great, 74

"Waits," 40
Wales, 63
Walnut shells, 30
Wassailing, 33, 42, 83
Weather forecasting, 55
Weihnacht, 13
Weir, Robert W., 24
Weiser, Francis X., 26, 75, 79
Wenceslaus, 28
Wernecke, Herbert H., 28
Wessex, 37
West Point, N. Y., 24
Wheat, sheaves of, 73
Williamsburg, Va., 21
Wise Men, 25, 42, 69, 74, 79, 83, 90, 97, 99, 104, 113, 115, 116, 118
Wood carving, 51
World War II, 48, 70
Wreath, 53, 104
Wren, 62

Xmas, meaning of, 13

Yorkshire, England, 36
Yule, 13, 14, 33, 51, 70, 84
Yule log, 33, 36, 42, 44, 72, 79
"Yule Man," 31
Yule Tree, 51, 87

Zampogne, 69
Zurich, 90, 94

LAKEWOOD MEMORIAL LIBRARY
LAKEWOOD, NEW YORK 14750

3 2005 0079884 6

J   7-DAY CHRISTMAS
394.268
F   Foley
     Christmas the world over

Date Due   C. 1

DEC 11 '72	DEC 26	NOV 17 '89	DEC 19 '94
DEC 26 '7	SEP 16 '80	DEC 06 '89	DEC 09
DEC 18 '7	330	DEC 5 '89	DEC 0 9 1997
JAN 2 '74	DEC 4 '81	DEC 13 '8	DEC 0 9 1997
DEC 16 74	DEC 20	JAN 19 '90	DEC 11
DEC 24 '75	DEC 28 8	DEC 7	DEC 29
DEC 14 '7	DEC 26 8	DEC 18 '9	Feb 09-0
DEC 15 '77	DEC 26 '8		DEC 18 2000
JAN 4 '78	DEC 14	DEC 23 '9	NOV 1 5 2002
JAN 2 '7	DEC 12 '88	NOV 2 6 2002	
DEC 8 '7	DEC 19 '88	DEC 1 2 '9	

LO: 11/02
ØXII
ØP+

LAKEWOOD MEMORIAL LIBRARY
LAKEWOOD, NEW YORK 14750

WITHDRAWN

Member Of
Chautauqua-Cattaraugus Library System

PRINTED IN U.S.A.